S

MW00975305

PASS TRAK® 63

License Exam Manual
Questions & Answers

Uniform Securities

Agent

State Law Exam

*14*th Edition

Dearborn
Financial Institute, Inc.®

At press time, this 14th edition of PASSTRAK® Series 63 contains the most complete and accurate information currently available for the NASAA Series 63 license examination. Owing to the nature of securities license examinations, however, information may have been added recently to the actual test that does not appear in this edition.

This publication is designed to provide accurate and authoritative information in regard to the subject matter covered. It is sold with the understanding that the publisher is not engaged in rendering legal, accounting or other professional service. If legal advice or other expert assistance is required, the services of a competent professional person should be sought.

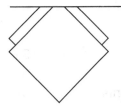

Contents

Acknowledgments

My thanks to each person who has contributed time and expertise for this 14th edition of *PASSTRAK*® *Series 63*. In particular, I wish to thank Marcia Burak, Phil Keener and the Answer Phone staff, who reviewed the text for technical accuracy, and Stuart Egrin, who collaborated on the review, research and development of *PASSTRAK*® *Series 63*, 14th edition.

Joan M. McGillivray, Editor

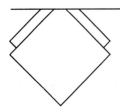

Introduction

Welcome to *PASSTRAK® Series 63*. Because you probably have a lot of questions about the course and the exams, we have tried to anticipate some of them and provide you with answers to help you on your way.

The Course

How is the course structured?

PASSTRAK® Series 63 License Exam Manual and Questions & Answers consists of text chapters and exam sets. Chapter 1 addresses the regulation and registration requirements for broker-dealers and agents at both the federal and state levels. Chapter 2 details regulation and registration requirements for investment advisers at federal and state levels. Chapter 3 covers requirements for registration and regulation of new issues. Chapter 4 focuses on the North American Securities Administrators Association's policies on unethical practices and on those portions of other federal securities acts necessary to pass the Uniform Securities Agent State Law Exam (the Series 63). Each chapter of text is devoted to those study areas with which you need to become familiar.

The remaining chapters consist of a review exam (chapter 5) and final exams (chapters 6 through 9) composed of questions similar to those you will encounter on the Series 63 test.

How much time should I spend studying?

You should plan to spend approximately 15 to 20 hours reading the material and working through the questions. Your actual time, of course, may vary from this figure depending on your reading rate, comprehension, professional background and study environment.

Spread your study time over the four to six days prior to the date on which you are scheduled to take the Series 63 exam. Select a time and place for studying that will allow you to concentrate your full attention on the material at hand. You have a lot of information to learn and a lot of ground to cover. Be sure to give yourself enough time to learn the material.

What is the best way to approach the exams?

Approach each review and final exam as if you were preparing to take the actual Series 63 test. Read each question carefully and write down your answer. Then check your answers against the key and read the accompanying rationale. Making yourself go through all of these steps (rather than simply reading each question and skipping directly to the rationale) will greatly increase your comprehension and retention of the information in the book.

Do I need to take all of the exams?

The exams test the same knowledge you will need in order to answer the questions on the NASD Series 63 exam. By completing all the exams and checking your answers against the rationale, you should be able to pinpoint any areas with which you are still having difficulty. Review any questions you miss, paying particular attention to the rationale for those questions. If any subjects still seem troublesome, go back and review the section(s) covering those topics. At the end of each rationale, you will find a page reference that directs you to the page in the text portion where the information is covered.

The Exam

Why do I need to pass the Series 63 exam?

Most states require securities agents to pass a qualification exam in order to become registered. To be registered to sell securities or to give investment advice in those states that require Series 63 qualification, you must pass the Series 63 exam.

What is the Series 63 exam like?

The Series 63 is a one-hour, 50-question exam administered by the NASD. It is offered as a computer-based test at various testing sites around the country. A pencil-and-paper exam is available to those candidates who apply to and obtain permission from the NASD to take a written exam.

What topics will I see covered on the exam?

This course covers the wide range of topics that the North American Securities Administrators Association (NASAA) has outlined as essential to the Uniform Securities Agent. The NASAA exam is divided into five broad topic areas:

Definitions of terms	20%
Licensing or registration requirements of broker-dealers	15%
Registration of securities, exempt securities and exempt transactions	10%
Fraudulent and other prohibited transactions	45%
Regulatory oversight, criminal penalties, civil liabilities, scope of the act and general provisions	10%

What score must I achieve in order to pass?

You must answer correctly at least 70% of the questions on the Series 63 exam in order to pass and become eligible for registration as a Uniform Securities Agent.

How long does the exam take?

You will be allowed one hour in which to finish the exam. If you are taking the computerized version of the exam, you will be given additional time before the test to become familiar with the PROCTOR® terminal.

Are there any prerequisites I have to meet before taking the exam?

There are no prerequisite exams you must pass before sitting for the Series 63.

How do I enroll for the exam?

To obtain an admission ticket to the Series 63 exam, your firm must file the proper application form with the NASD, along with the appropriate processing fees. The NASD will then send you a directory of Certification Testing Centers and a PROCTOR® enrollment valid for a stated number of days. To take the exam during this period, you must make an appointment with a Certification Testing Center as far in advance as possible of the date on which you would like to sit for the test.

What should I take to the exam?

Take one form of personal identification that bears your signature and your photograph as issued by a government agency. You are not allowed to take reference materials or anything else into the testing area. Calculators are available upon request; you will not be allowed to use your personal calculator.

Scratch paper and pencils will be provided by the testing center, although you will not be permitted to take them with you when you leave.

What is PROCTOR®?

The Series 63 exam, like many professional licensing examinations, is administered on the PROCTOR® computerized testing system. PROCTOR® is a nationwide, interactive computer system designed for the administration and delivery of qualifications examinations. Included with your PROCTOR® enrollment, you will receive a brochure describing how the exam is formatted and how to use the computer terminal to answer the questions.

When you have completed the exam, the PROCTOR® system promptly scores your answers and within minutes displays your grade for the exam on the terminal screen.

How well can I expect to do on the exam?

The examinations administered by the NASD are not easy. You will be required to display considerable understanding and knowledge of the topics presented in this course in order to pass the Series 63 exam and qualify for registration. If you study and complete all of the sections of the course, and consistently score at least 80% on the exams, you should be well prepared to pass the Series 63 exam.

1 Regulation and Registration of Broker-Dealers and Agents

Key Terms	administrator	sales representative
	advertising	Securities Act of 1933
	agent	Securities Exchange Act of 1934
	blue-sky laws	securities information processor
	broker-dealer	security
	institutional investor	surety bond
	Investment Company Act of 1940	transfer agent
	offer	underwriter
	person	Uniform Securities Act (USA)
	rescission	

Overview

The securities industry is regulated at both the federal and the state levels. These regulations govern how securities are issued, registered, sold and traded, as well as who may perform these activities. At the federal level, the principal acts that regulate the industry are the Securities Act of 1933 and the Securities Exchange Act of 1934. The focus of the National Securities Markets Improvement Act of 1996 regarding broker-dealers and agents is the prevention of abuse of the public trust in sales and trading practices. These provisions were adopted under the Uniform Securities Act.

The basis for industry regulation at the state level is the Uniform Securities Act (USA); this is model legislation that each state may adopt in its entirety or may, within certain limits, adapt to suit its needs. Each state appoints a state securities administrator, who is vested with certain powers under the USA.

This chapter describes both state and federal regulation of broker-dealers and agents.

Overview of Securities Trading Regulation

Definitions

Accredited investor. As defined in Rule 502 of Regulation D of the Securities Act of 1933, an accredited investor is any institution (such as a bank, a broker-dealer or an investment company) or any individual meeting minimum net worth requirements for the purchase of securities qualifying under the Regulation D registration exemption.

An accredited investor, also called a *professional*, a *sophisticated* or an *institutional investor*, generally is accepted to be one who has:

- a net worth of $1 million or more; or
- had an annual income of $200,000 or more in each of the two most recent years (or $300,000 jointly with a spouse) and who has a reasonable expectation of reaching the same income level in the current year.

Agent. An agent, also called a *sales representative*, is an individual who acts for the accounts of others. The Uniform Securities Act gives the term "agent" special meanings. "Agent" is defined as an individual who represents a broker-dealer or an issuer when selling or trying to sell securities to the investing public. This individual is considered an agent whether he actually receives or simply solicits orders. In other words, an agent is anyone who accepts an order and receives compensation while representing a broker-dealer or an issuer.

Associated person. An associated person includes any partner, branch manager, officer or director of a broker-dealer, including outside directors. It also includes employees such as sales representatives who are not clerks or ministerial personnel, as well as anyone who controls, is controlled by or is under common control with the broker-dealer.

Broker-dealer. A broker-dealer is any person with an established place of business who engages in the business of effecting securities transactions for the accounts of others or for his own account. Broker-dealers must be licensed (registered) in a state to transact business in that state.

Equity security. An equity security is any kind of stock—common or preferred, for example—or any security that allows someone to acquire stock, either through a right or warrant to purchase stock or through a conversion privilege. Bonds are not equity securities, but if they are issued with a warrant to purchase stock or are convertible into stock, they fall under the definition of an equity security in the 1934 act.

Government security. The 1934 act defines government securities as those issued or guaranteed by the U.S. government or one of its agencies. Securities issued or guaranteed by a state, county or city or any agency of a nonfederal governmental unit are municipal securities.

Government securities dealer. A government securities dealer is any dealer that effects transactions in government securities exclusively.

Guaranteed. Under the USA, the term "guarantee" indicates that a person (such as an insurance company or the U.S. government) has assumed responsibility for the payment of a security's principal, interest or dividends, as specified by the guarantee.

Institutional investor. An institutional investor is a person or an organization that trades for itself or for others in a fiduciary capacity and typically trades securities in large enough share quantities or dollar amounts that it qualifies for preferential treatment and lower trade costs (commissions). However, no minimum investment amount is set for institutional transactions. Institutional investors are covered by fewer protective regulations because it is assumed that they are more knowledgeable and better able to protect themselves.

Institutional investors include:

- investment companies
- insurance companies
- investment advisers
- broker-dealers
- banks
- trust companies
- savings and loan associations
- employee benefits programs with assets of at least $1 million
- government agencies

Issuer (underwriter). Any person who issues or proposes to issue a security is considered an issuer under the USA.

Market maker. A dealer willing to accept the risk of holding securities to facilitate trading in a particular security(ies) is a market maker.

Offer and sell. To understand the rules relating to the sale and purchase of securities, it is important to understand the difference between *offering to sell* a security and *selling* a security. An offer is an indication by an investor, a trader or a dealer of a willingness to sell a security or commodity. Under the Uniform Securities Act, every attempt to solicit a purchase or sale in a security *for money or other value* constitutes an offer. The term "sell," on the other hand, means the act of conveying ownership of a security or other property for money or other value and includes every contract to sell a security or an interest in a security. In addition to the everyday usage of the term "sell," sales also include the following:

- Any security given or delivered with or as a bonus for any purchase of securities is considered to have been offered and sold for value.
- A gift of assessable stock is considered to involve an offer and a sale.
- Every sale or offer of a warrant or right to purchase or subscribe to another security is considered to include an offer of the other security.

The definition of "sale" does not include a stock dividend if nothing of value is given by the stockholders for the dividend. The definition also does not include a bona fide pledge or loan, such as a broker-dealer's loan of securities to a customer.

Securities information processor. The 1934 act defines a securities information processor as a person who is in the business of providing information about securities transactions or quotations on a current and continuing basis. The information may be published on paper (such as in the *Pink Sheets*), or it may be disseminated through a computer network (such as the Dow Jones Wire News) or another communications system. However, persons who handle such information on a regular basis in the course of their business activities—such as a radio or television station—but who are not "in the business" of doing so are specifically excluded from the definition of "securities information processor."

Security. Under the USA and the acts of 1933 and 1934, any note, stock, bond, investment contract, debenture, certificate of interest in a profit-sharing or partnership agreement, certificate of deposit, collateral trust certificate, preorganization certificate, option on a security, or other instrument of investment commonly known as a *security* is considered a security.

The accurate determination of what is a security is crucial to registered representatives conducting their activities in compliance with state securities laws. In general, "security" can be defined as any piece of securitized paper that can be traded for value.

As established by the federal courts, the basic test for determining whether a specific investment falls within the definition of a security is whether the person invests her money in a common enterprise and is led to expect profits from the managerial efforts of the promoter or a third party. Thus, the definition of "security" also includes interests in the following: oil and gas drilling programs, real estate condominiums and cooperatives, farmland or animals, commodity option contracts (but not the underlying futures contracts), whiskey warehouse receipts, insurance company separate accounts, multilevel distributorship arrangements and merchandising marketing programs.

Exemptions from the definition of "security" are insurance policies; endowment contracts; fixed annuities; retirement plans that serve as vehicles for other investments; checking, savings or passbook accounts; and preliminary or final prospectuses.

Transfer agent. A transfer agent is a person or an organization responsible for recording the names of registered stockholders and the number of shares owned, seeing that the certificates are signed by the appropriate corporate officers, affixing the corporate seal and delivering the securities to the transferee. A firm that effects shareholder requests to convert mutual fund shares on behalf of the mutual fund would be considered a transfer agent. Clearing agencies performing the functions of a transfer agent with respect to contracts they issue and insurance companies are specifically excluded from the act of 1934 definition of "transfer agent."

The Securities Exchange Act of 1934

After the Securities Act of 1933 was enacted regulating primary issues of securities, attention turned to the need for regulating secondary trading. One purpose of the Securities Exchange Act of 1934 is to maintain a fair market for the investing public. It seeks to attain this goal by regulating the securities exchanges and the over-the-counter (OTC) markets. Commonly called the **Exchange Act**, it formed the SEC and gave the Commission authority to oversee the securities markets and to register and regulate the exchanges.

The Securities Exchange Act of 1934, which has much greater breadth than the act of 1933, addresses the:

- creation of the SEC;
- registration and regulation of the exchanges and their members;
- regulation of credit (through the margin requirements set by the Federal Reserve Board—FRB);
- registration of broker-dealers that trade securities on national exchanges or OTC;
- registration of persons who effect securities transactions with the public;
- regulation of insider transactions, short sales and proxies;
- regulation of trading activities;
- regulation of client accounts;
- customer protection rule;
- regulation of the self-regulatory organizations (SROs)—for example, the National Association of Securities Dealers, the New York Stock Exchange and the Municipal Securities Rulemaking Board;
- regulation of the OTC market; and
- net capital requirements for broker-dealers.

The Securities and Exchange Commission

The SEC, created by the act of 1934, was given responsibility and authority to regulate the securities markets. The SEC is made up of five commissioners appointed by the President of the United States and approved by the Senate. SEC commissioners appointed under the act of 1934 may have no business or employment other than their commission's, and may not engage in securities trading during their terms. One of the group's primary responsibilities is to enforce the act of 1934.

The SEC has established rules regarding net capital requirements for broker-dealers, hypothecation (pledging) of customers' securities, commingling (mixing) of broker-dealer securities with those of customers, the use of manipulative and deceptive devices and broker-dealer recordkeeping. The SEC enforces the Securities Exchange Act of 1934 and others by providing rules and prescribing penalties for violations.

The SROs, such as the NASD, are required to assist the SEC by establishing rules and trade practices that member firms must follow. The SROs are empowered by law to enforce both federal law and their own rules.

Expansion of the SEC's Role

The National Securities Markets Improvement Act of 1996 enhanced the SEC's role to include improvement and oversight of (1) market efficiency, (2) competition in the securities industry, (3) capital formation and (4) elimination of regulations that no longer serve the public interest.

Jurisdiction of the SEC

As discussed earlier, the 1934 act formed the SEC and gave the Commission authority to oversee the securities markets and self-regulatory organizations such as the NASD, the MSRB and the NYSE. The SEC has the power to administer federal and SRO laws relating to the securities industry, and to investigate violations of those laws. The SEC's jurisdiction does not extend to violations of banking rules. The Commission has preemptive authority over the rules established by the Uniform Securities Act or state securities administrators.

The jurisdiction of the SEC was greatly enhanced by changes to federal securities law enacted as the National Securities Markets Improvement Act of 1996.

Registration of Exchanges and Corporations

Under the 1934 act, a "securities exchange" is any entity in the business of providing the facilities and means for buyers and sellers to transact business in securities. The national securities exchanges must file registration statements with the SEC. When they register, the exchanges agree to comply with and help enforce the rules of this act. Registered broker-dealers are prohibited from effecting transactions on any exchange that is not registered with the SEC.

Each exchange gives the SEC copies of its bylaws, constitution and articles of incorporation. Any amendment to rules must be disclosed as soon as it is adopted. The exchange must also institute and enforce disciplinary procedures for members who do not use just and equitable practices. Small local exchanges are exempt from registration.

The SEC may suspend all trading on an exchange if it has cause to believe that the suspension would be in the public good and if it notifies the President of the United States.

In addition to the registration of exchanges, the act of 1934 requires companies that list securities on those exchanges to register with the SEC. Each listed company must file quarterly statements on Form 10Q and annual statements on Form 10K informing the SEC of its financial status as well as other information.

Many firms with securities traded OTC must also register. Those firms with 500 or more stockholders and assets of $5 million or more are required to do so. Exchange members who do business with the public also must register with the SEC, as well as broker-dealers that do business OTC or that use the mail or other *instruments of interstate commerce* (telephone, television, radio, etc.) to conduct OTC business.

The Maloney Act, an amendment to the Securities Exchange Act of 1934, permitted the establishment of a national securities association of broker-dealers transacting business in the OTC market. According to the act, SROs such as the NASD could be established and registered with the SEC.

Extension of Credit in the Securities Industry

The Federal Reserve Board, established by Congress in 1913, is composed of seven members appointed by the President of the United States and confirmed by the Senate to serve 14-year terms.

The FRB regulates the extension of credit (**margin**) in the industry through **Regulation T (Reg T)**. To prevent the excessive use of credit to buy securities, the FRB sets the minimum margin a customer must deposit (expressed as a percentage of purchase price) when purchasing securities from a broker-dealer or when selling securities short. Currently, the required minimum deposit is 50 percent of the securities' market value at the time of purchase.

Reg T requires that a customer pay for purchases in a cash account or make deposits in a margin account within two business days after the end of the regular way settlement cycle unless an SRO has granted an extension. (Currently, regular way settlement takes place on the third day after the trade date.)

Certain securities are exempt from the Reg T initial margin requirement, including U.S. government securities and municipal bonds. Other securities are not eligible for purchase on margin—for example, new issues of securities (within the first 30 days of issuance) and over-the-counter securities that the FRB has not designated as marginable.

Changes to federal securities law enacted under the National Securities Markets Improvement Act of 1996 eased restrictions regarding the financing of new issues (primary offerings) by loans from commercial banks to broker-dealers acting as underwriters.

Overview of the Uniform Securities Act

State Securities Laws

In addition to federal securities regulations, each state has laws that pertain to the trading of securities in the secondary market. State securities laws are known as **blue-sky laws**. The term "blue-sky" was first used by a Kansas Supreme Court justice, who referred to "speculative schemes that have no more basis than so many feet of blue sky." The Uniform Securities Act serves as model legislation that each state may follow or adapt to its own needs.

Kansas was the first state in the Union to adopt a comprehensive licensing system pertaining to securities and individuals engaged in the securities business. That law passed in 1911. Within two years, 23 states had followed this state's leadership and had enacted similar laws. By 1933, the blue-sky movement had spread to 47 of the 48 states then in the Union, as well as to the territory of Hawaii.

Through the years, many attempts were made to devise a uniform act to regulate the sale of securities. In 1954, the National Conference of Commissioners on Uniform State Laws commissioned an examination of the problem and a detailed analysis of the numerous existing laws and judicial decisions. The result, after two years of intensive study, was the **Uniform Securities Act** (**USA**).

This act has gained wide acceptance throughout the nation, simplifying and improving greatly the functioning of professionals within the securities industry.

Administration of the Uniform Securities Act

Scope of the act. The Uniform Securities Act gives each state's state securities administrator (sometimes known as the *state securities commissioner* or *state securities secretary*) the power to enforce the act in that state. The administrator has jurisdiction over any offer to buy or sell and any acceptance of an offer to buy or sell securities if the offer is:

- originated in the administrator's state
- directed to that state
- accepted in that state

This regulation means that any offer of a security is subject to the rules of the state administrator of the state in which the offer was made and of the state to which the offer was directed or in which the offer was accepted. The state from which payment is made or to which securities are delivered is not considered important.

A distinction must be made here, however. An advertisement of an offer that is placed in a newspaper or magazine, or that is broadcast on radio or television, is considered an offer *only in the state of publication or broadcast*. This interpretation of the act provides some protection for the offeror under those circumstances where the offeror's control over who receives the offer is limited. As an example, a person may advertise an offer in the *Chicago Tribune* and not be liable for subscriptions mailed to residents of states where the security is not registered. Also, an advertisement placed in a national publication is not considered an offer in the state where the newspaper or magazine is published if more than two-thirds of its circulation is outside the state. The offeror would, however, be responsible for determining whether an offer to purchase that comes from another state meets that state's requirements before it is accepted.

State Securities Administrators

The Uniform Securities Act sets forth the requirements for appointing state securities administrators. The act provides for minimum official behavior and conduct requirements, such as prohibitions against an administrator's using his position for personal benefit, disclosing confidential information and so on.

Administrators are permitted to establish broker-dealer and agent registration, testing, filing and fee regulations as would be appropriate to their states' requirements. In addition to mandating the registration of firms and associated persons, most states require that securities be registered in those states before they can be sold to the public. The Uniform Securities Act gives administrators the right to deny, suspend or revoke the registrations of broker-dealers, agents, investment advisers and securities if the administrators have just reason to do so under the rules of the act.

The USA also provides for criminal penalties and civil liabilities for persons involved in illegal securities transactions and prescribes the limits of a state's jurisdiction.

Investigations and Subpoenas

The administrator has the authority to inspect a broker-dealer and to conduct investigations to determine whether persons have violated or are about to violate the provisions of the Uniform Securities Act. These investigations may be private or public, and they may take place in the administrator's state.

The administrator also has the power to administer oaths, subpoena persons to testify, compel them to produce records or to attend hearings in connection with investigations. The administrator may delegate another official to carry out these functions only. Should a person who has been subpoenaed demonstrate *contumacy* (contempt for the administrator's order), or if a person ignores a subpoena, the administrator may ask a court to enforce the order. A person demonstrating contumacy risks punishment for contempt of court.

The Fifth Amendment—refusal to give information or assistance in an administrator's investigation because of possible self-incrimination—cannot be applied under the USA.

Penalties under the USA

If the administrator suspects that a person has engaged in or is about to engage in an activity that violates the act, the administrator may issue a cease and desist order without a prior hearing or may bring an action against that person in an appropriate court.

Criminal penalties. Persons found guilty of willful violations of the Uniform Securities Act are subject to criminal penalties. Upon conviction, a person may be fined up to $5,000, imprisoned not more than three years or both. In criminal matters, the statute of limitations runs for five years. The Investment Advisers Act of 1940 allows for a maximum fine of $10,000, imprisonment for not more than five years or both.

Civil liabilities. If a sale of a security has violated the provisions of the Uniform Securities Act, the buyer may sue to:

- recover the money he paid for the security from the person who sold that security to him; and
- receive interest on his money from the date of the purchase. (Any income the buyer received while he owned the security is deducted from the interest the seller paid.)

Under the Uniform Securities Act, the seller is not necessarily the only person held liable for a fraudulent sale of securities. The seller's supervisor or employer, who directly or indirectly controls the seller's activities, may also be subject to civil penalties, and liability may also extend to any other employee who assisted the seller materially. In addition, the seller may be held liable for court costs and reasonable attorney's fees.

Right of rescission. If the seller discovers that he has made an illegal sale, he may offer to repurchase the security from the buyer. To satisfy the buyer's rights of rescission, the amount paid to the buyer must include the purchase price and interest, as set by the administrator.

Statute of limitations. The buyer of a security or the receiver of investment advice may not sue for compensation more than two years after discovering the violation or three years after the act or transaction that constituted the violation, whichever occurs first. The buyer may not sue either if, when he still owned the security, he received a written offer from the seller to refund the money and interest and failed to accept the offer within 30 days. The act also contains settlement provisions for buyers who already have disposed of the stock before a settlement is offered.

Registration of Broker-Dealers and Agents

Federal Registration of Broker-Dealers

According to the Securities Exchange Act of 1934, exchange members and broker-dealers that trade securities OTC and on exchanges and individuals who effect securities trades with the public must register with the SEC.

Exemptions. Exemptions from registration include any broker-dealer that deals only on an intrastate basis. The intrastate exemption is available to a broker-dealer whose business is conducted exclusively in one state and that does not make use of national securities exchanges. An *intra*state firm, however, cannot use the mail or other instruments of *inter*state commerce and still qualify for the exemption from registration.

Statutory disqualification from registration. Administrative sanctions, court injunctions and findings of criminal wrongdoing are causes for statutory disqualification from registration with the SEC and association with any SRO.

State Registration of Broker-Dealers

Most states require broker-dealers that do business in a particular state to register with that state's securities commission or administrator. Agents associated with a broker-dealer also must be registered in the state(s) where they do business. The state securities administrator has the power to revoke a broker-dealer's registration or an agent's license if the firm or representative has violated any of the state's securities laws.

The Uniform Securities Act establishes specific licensing and registration requirements and procedures for broker-dealers and agents. The act also prescribes certain post-licensing provisions.

Under the USA, it is unlawful for any person to transact business in a state as a broker-dealer or an agent unless the person is registered under the Uniform Securities Act or is exempt from registration.

Exemptions from state registration. Agents, issuers, banks, savings institutions and trust companies are exempt from registering as broker-dealers in the states where they conduct business. The definition of "broker-dealer" also exempts persons who transact business exclusively with issuers, depository institutions, trust companies, insurance companies, investment companies, pension or profit-sharing plans, financial institutions or institutional buyers.

A broker-dealer is not subject to state registration requirements if it conducts business in a state with an existing client who has less than 30 days' temporary residence in the state. The exemption allows a broker-dealer to serve the needs of an existing client who is vacationing in a state where the broker-dealer is not registered. This registration exemption was adopted from the National Securities Markets Improvement Act (NSMIA).

Agent Registration

A broker-dealer may not employ a person as an agent unless that person is registered (or exempt). It is unlawful for any person to transact business in any state as an agent unless that person is registered under the Uniform Securities Act or is exempt from registration. The person must be registered as an agent even if the securities or the transactions involved in a particular offer or sale are exempt from registration requirements.

Exemptions from state registration. Agents must be licensed (registered) in a state to transact business there. However, certain classes of agents are exempt from the registration requirements.

An agent is not required to register if he represents (is employed by) only the following exempt *issuers*:

- U.S. government;
- municipality;
- Canadian government, province or municipality (but not a Canadian corporation);
- any foreign government with which the United States maintains diplomatic relations; or
- depository institution, savings institution or trust company.

An agent is not required to register if he represents only the following exempt *securities*:

- promissory note, draft or banker's acceptance with a maturity of nine months or less; or
- investment contract issued in connection with an employee's stock purchase, savings, pension, profit-sharing or similar benefit plan.

Finally, an agent is not required to register if:

- he represents an issuer in an exempt *transaction*; or
- as a partner, an officer or a director of a brokerage firm, he limits his activities to managerial functions and does not attempt to effect purchases or sales. (He is not considered an agent merely because he is a partner, an officer or a director of a brokerage firm.)

Length of Registration

Every registration of a broker-dealer or an agent expires annually on December 31st unless renewed.

State Registration Procedures

Application. A broker-dealer or an agent may obtain an initial or a renewal registration by filing (1) an application with (2) the appropriate filing fee, as set by each state, and (3) a consent to service of process with the administrator in the form the administrator requires.

A consent to service of process gives the administrator the irrevocable right to receive and process, as the applicant's attorney, any legal complaints that may arise in regard to an applicant's conduct as an agent or a broker-dealer. Once the applicant has filed the consent to service of process, any complaint presented to the administrator has the same force and validity as if it had been served personally on the applicant.

An application for any registration must contain whatever information the administrator requires concerning such matters as the applicant's:

- form and place of business organization;
- proposed method of doing business;
- qualifications and business history, including those of any partner, director or similar person of a broker-dealer;
- history of injunctions, conviction of any felony or conviction of any misdemeanor involving any aspect of the securities business; and
- financial condition and history.

The administrator may also require an applicant for initial registration to publish an announcement of the registration application in one or more specific newspapers in the state.

If the administrator does not deny the registration or is not in the process of denying the registration, that registration becomes effective at noon of the 30th day after the application is filed. The administrator may allow an earlier effective date. He also may defer the effective date until noon of the 30th day after the filing of any amendment.

Financial requirements. The administrator may set minimum capital requirements for broker-dealers registered in the state. Broker-dealers in compliance with the SEC's net capital requirements are exempt from the USA's minimum capital requirements.

Surety bonds. Broker-dealers and agents may be required by the administrator to post **surety bonds** if the person has custody of or discretionary authority over customer funds or securities. Typically, surety bonds are set in amounts of $35,000, although deposits of cash or securities may be permissible instead of the bonds. Compliance with minimum capital requirements releases the person from the surety bond requirement.

Qualification examinations. The administrator may require that one or more officers or agents of the broker-dealer take an examination that may be written, oral or both.

Successful completion of the Uniform Securities Agent State Law Examination (Series 63), the Uniform Investment Adviser Law Examination (Series 65), the Uniform Combined State Law Examination (Series 66) or any of the NASD, New York Stock Exchange (NYSE) or Municipal Securities Rulemaking Board (MSRB) examinations does not automatically constitute registration in a state. An applicant who has passed the exam does not have the right to transact business until the state administrator has granted his registration. Before granting an agent's initial registration, some states may require that the applicant, his firm or both provide additional certification showing that the applicant has reviewed his state's blue-sky laws and understands his responsibilities.

Responsibilities of those who pass the examination. Successful completion of the Series 63, Series 65 or Series 66 does not relieve the agent of the following responsibilities:

- to know and abide by the specific requirements of the securities laws and requirements of regulations of the states in which he will transact business;
- to understand that he does not have the right to transact business before a state grants his license or registration; and
- to know that some states may require further certification to indicate that he has reviewed his state's blue-sky laws and understands his responsibilities.

Employment. No broker-dealer or issuer can lawfully employ an agent unless that agent is registered. Conversely, an agent is not effectively registered unless he is employed by a registered broker-dealer or issuer. This means that an agent's registration is not considered to be in effect during any period when the agent is not employed by a broker-dealer, even if the agent's nonassociation is temporary, such as when the agent is between employers.

Changes in employment. Whenever an agent begins or terminates employment with an employer, the agent as well as the employer must promptly notify the administrator.

When an agent transfers his employment from one broker-dealer or issuer to another, all three persons—the agent, the former employer and the new employer—must notify the administrator.

A termination becomes effective 30 days after the state administrator receives the notice, but may be postponed if a suspension or revocation proceeding is pending. After the termination becomes effective, the administrator retains the right to suspend or revoke registration for one year.

Firm registration. At the time a broker-dealer is registered, anyone who is then a partner, an officer or a director of the broker-dealer is automatically registered as an agent if that person acts in the capacity of an agent and not otherwise. Silent partners are not considered agents because they do not act in the capacity of agents.

If a person becomes a partner, an officer or a director of a broker-dealer after the broker-dealer's registration date, that individual is not automatically registered as an agent, even if he acts as one. If an individual is an officer of a broker-dealer at the time the broker-dealer is registered, and if that individual acts in the capacity of an agent and therefore is considered registered as an agent, he need not take an additional examination.

If a registered broker-dealer intends to cease doing business as such and to pass its registration on to a successor firm, such as in the event of a merger, an acquisition or a sale of the business, it must file an application for registration of the successor firm, even if the successor firm is not yet in existence. The term of the new registration begins on the date the original firm ceases to do business. The filing fee is waived for the successor's initial registration application.

Denial, Suspension or Revocation of Registration

All registrations required by the Uniform Securities Act fall under the state administrators' jurisdiction. An administrator may deny, suspend or revoke any registration, or bar or censure any registrant, or restrict or limit any registrant's functions or activities if he finds that the:

- order is in the public interest; *and*
- the applicant, registrant or issuer of a security is guilty of any of a specified list of offenses.

Among these offenses are the following:

- filing an incomplete, false or misleading application for registration;
- willfully violating any provision of the Uniform Securities Act;
- being convicted of a misdemeanor involving any aspect of the securities business or being convicted of any felony within the past 10 years;
- being temporarily or permanently enjoined from engaging in the securities business by a court of law;
- being subject to an order of the administrator denying, suspending or revoking registration;
- violating any federal or state securities or commodities law within the past 10 years;
- engaging in dishonest or unethical securities practices;
- insolvency;
- having willfully violated securities or banking laws of a foreign jurisdiction or, within the past five years, being subject to an action of a foreign securities regulator denying, suspending or revoking the right to conduct securities business;
- being discovered not to be qualified on the basis of training, experience or knowledge;
- being in a supervisory position and failing to supervise registered employees; or
- failing to pay application filing fees.

Denial of registration due to lack of qualification. The administrator may deny, revoke or suspend any applicant's registration because that person is not qualified due to lack of knowledge, training or experience. However, the administrator may not base the decision solely on lack of experience. In the same way, the administrator may not deny, revoke or suspend the registration of a firm (broker-dealer or investment adviser) based solely on its representatives' lack of experience.

The act authorizes the administrator to restrict a particular applicant's registration to that of a broker-dealer if the administrator finds the individual is not qualified as an investment adviser. Experience is a consideration, but lack of experience cannot be the sole factor for denying registration.

A representative is not required to meet the same level of qualification as the broker-dealer or investment adviser for which he works. A person registered and with experience as a broker-dealer or an agent is not necessarily qualified to be registered as an investment adviser. The broker-dealer may be prohibited from transacting business in any state as an investment adviser until such time as it does become registered.

Canadian Firms and Agents

Registration exemption. A Canadian broker-dealer may conduct business in a state without registering under the USA if it has an office in Canada, has no office in the state and conducts business exclusively with established customers or with financial institutions. The same registration exemption applies to Canadian agents.

Simplified registration. If a Canadian broker-dealer or agent is not exempt from registration, the USA provides a simplified registration process. If it is registered in Canada and is a member of a Canadian self-regulatory organization, a broker-dealer may register by filing an application and a consent to service of process. An agent registered in Canada may register by filing the same materials. The registrations become effective 30 days after filing.

Additional requirements. Each Canadian broker-dealer must maintain its Canadian registration and exchange membership in good standing; provide its books and records to the state administrator upon request; inform the administrator of any sanction or regulatory action entered against it; and disclose to its customers in the state that it is not subject to all USA requirements.

A Canadian broker-dealer or agent registered under the USA must file annual renewal applications and pay the appropriate filing fees. It is subject to all of the USA's antifraud provisions.

Federal and State Laws Regarding Broker-Dealers

Table 1.1 compares the federal and state laws and regulations regarding broker-dealers.

Table 1.1   Comparison of Federal and State Laws Regarding Broker-Dealers

Item	Federal Law	State Law
Definition	A person engaged in the business of effecting securities transactions for the accounts of others or for its own account.	A person who effects transactions for the accounts of others or for its own account.
Exclusions	Bank.	Agent; issuer; bank; savings institution; trust company.
Exemptions	Business is exclusively in one state and does not make use of any national securities exchange.	No place of business within the state and directs an offer in the state to an existing customer who has less than *30 days'* temporary residency in the state. Clients are limited to issuers, other broker-dealers, depository institutions, trust companies, investment companies, employee benefit plans, other financial institutions.
Registration	File application on Form BD with the SEC; effective 45 days after filing.	File application, consent to service of process and fee; effective on the 30th day after filing.
Length of Registration	Effective until withdrawn, revoked or canceled.	Expires every December 31st unless renewed.
Withdrawal of Registration	Takes effect 60 days after filing Form BDW with the SEC.	Takes effect 30 days after filing.
Insolvency	Not cause for revocation.	Cause for revocation.
Records	Must be maintained for 3 years, 6 years or the life of the firm, depending on the type of record.	Must maintain records prescribed by administrator for 3 years.
Criminal Penalties	10 years in jail or $1 million fine; for other than a natural person, $2.5 million fine.	$5,000 fine or 3 years in jail.
Statute of Limitations	3 years after act or 1 year after discovery.	3 years after act or 2 years after discovery.

2 Regulation and Registration of Investment Advisers

Key Terms

agency cross transaction
assignment
bank
conditional exemption
contract
custody
de minimis exemption
disclosure brochure
fiduciary
foreign securities authority
Form ADV
impersonal advisory service

investment adviser
investment adviser representative
Investment Advisers Act of 1940
investment advisory contract
investment supervisory service
National Securities Markets
    Improvement Act of 1996
private investment company
qualified purchaser
supervised person
written disclosure statement

Overview

The regulation of investment advisers was deemed necessary when the growing profession became national in scope and grew to have far-reaching effects on the securities industry and its clientele's finances. Thus, the Investment Advisers Act of 1940 was enacted and many of its provisions adopted under the USA.

Among the important aspects of the Investment Advisers Act of 1940 are (1) the requirement that persons in the business of giving investment advice on a regular basis and charging a fee for the advice must register as investment advisers, and (2) the establishment of standards of ethical business conduct.

The National Securities Markets Improvement Act of 1996 (NSMIA) amends sections of the act of 1940 on a state level. The act has two major themes: (1) the restructuring of the division of responsibilities between the federal regulatory authorities and state securities administrators and (2) the enhancement of mutual fund regulation.

In addition, the National Securities Markets Improvement Act of 1996 provides for the efficient regulation of investment advisers. An investment adviser is regulated either by the SEC or by the state in which it conducts business.

Registration of Investment Advisers

A familiarity with the terms established by the Investment Advisers Act of 1940, also known as the *advisers act,* and SEC Release IA-1092 is important to an understanding of the act itself. Most of the definitions used in the act are similar to those set forth in other securities acts.

Definitions

Person. Although most people think of an individual when they hear the word "person," throughout securities law and this text the term "person" refers to any:

- individual
- corporation
- partnership
- association
- joint stock company
- trust where a security evidences the beneficiaries' interests
- unincorporated organization
- government or political subdivision of a government

Investment adviser. Any person who (1) provides investment advice, (2) is in the business of providing investment advice and (3) is compensated for providing investment advice is considered an **investment adviser**. Investment advisory services may be direct, such as during face-to-face financial planning, or impersonal, such as through an investment newsletter, an analysis, a report or an online computer service. For example, a certified financial planner who is compensated for his investment advice during the regular course of business is regarded as an investment adviser.

If the person giving the advice holds himself out as an investment adviser or receives any compensation for giving investment advice, the person is considered to be "in the business" of giving investment advice and must register under the act. For example, an athlete's business manager is regarded as being "in the business" if he is compensated and provides investment advice to the athlete.

Compensation for investment advice can take the form of a(n):

- advisory fee
- total services fee
- commission
- any combination of the above

The payments may be considered compensation even if not paid directly by the person receiving the investment advice. Compensation can come from another source, such as commissions generated from sales of the products the investment adviser has recommended.

The definition of "investment adviser" does *not* include:

- banks and bank holding companies;
- publishers of any bona fide newspaper, newsmagazine or business or financial publication of general and regular circulation (such as *The Wall Street Journal* or *Business Week*);

- brokers or dealers (or their associated persons and registered reps) whose giving of investment advice is incidental to the conduct of the broker-dealer's business and who receive no special compensation for the advice;
- persons who advise on U.S. government securities (federal level only); or
- persons whose giving of investment advice is incidental to their professions, such as:
  - lawyers
  - accountants
  - engineers
  - teachers

Investment adviser representative (supervised person). An investment adviser representative is any partner, officer, director or other individual directly or indirectly controlled by an investment adviser. An investment adviser rep is an individual who makes investment recommendations, manages customer accounts, solicits investment advisory services or supervises the employees who perform any of these duties. Clerical and ministerial personnel are not considered investment adviser reps.

Investment counsel. An investment adviser may use the term "investment counsel" to describe her business if her principal business consists of acting as an investment adviser and a substantial part of her business consists of rendering investment supervisory services.

Investment supervisory service. An investment adviser who gives continuous advice on the investment of funds on the basis of a customer's individual needs is said to be engaging in "investment supervisory services."

Impersonal advisory service. Any contract between an investment adviser and a client to provide investment advisory services that are not intended to meet directly the needs of a specific individual or account (such as an advisory newsletter or seminar) is considered a contract for "impersonal advisory services."

Administrator. The official or agency that administers the Uniform Securities Act in a state is known as the *administrator* or as the state securities *commissioner* or *secretary*.

Assignment. The term "assignment" signifies any direct or indirect transfer of an advisory contract or a controlling interest in an advisory contract. The term does not include a change in control based on the death of a partner or another member of an investment adviser. A transfer of control or ownership interest in an investment advisory contract is not considered an assignment if it does not result in an actual change in control or management.

Bank. A bank is any banking institution organized under the laws of the United States, any member of the Federal Reserve System or any other firm doing business as a bank under a state's laws.

Fiduciary. A person entrusted with the control of assets for another person (the beneficial owner) is considered a "fiduciary." The duties and responsibilities of fiduciaries are regulated by law in most states. In all cases, a fiduciary must act primarily for the benefit of his clients, exercise good faith and care in handling a beneficial owner's assets and make full and fair disclosure of all material facts.

One category of material facts that a fiduciary must disclose is any actual or potential conflicts of interest with a client. Conflicts of interest can take many forms, including:

- dual employment (such as an investment adviser who is also a registered representative of a broker-dealer or an associated person of an insurance company);
- personal transactions in securities that are affected by recommendations to clients (such as an investment adviser who holds options on a stock and who recommends that clients purchase that stock);
- any interest an investment adviser has in the securities about which he gives advice (such as being a controlling person of the issuer or receiving any form of compensation from the issuer for the recommendation of its securities); and
- any compensation that will be received from another source.

Private investment company. An unregistered investment company whose investment objective is to raise capital for business ventures is considered a private investment company. Investors in such a company are known as "qualified purchasers."

Foreign securities authority. Any foreign government, or any governmental body or regulatory organization empowered by a foreign government to regulate securities matters, is considered a "foreign securities authority."

Qualified purchaser. An investment sophisticate is considered a "qualified purchaser" if the investor is a(n):

- individual who owns $5 million or more in investments, including investments held jointly with a spouse;
- family-held business that owns $5 million or more in investments;
- business that has discretion over $25 million or more in investments; or
- trust sponsored by qualified purchasers.

North American Securities Administrators Association (NASAA). NASAA is a trade organization for state securities administrators of the United States, Canada and Mexico. Its purpose is to provide a medium for cooperation and coordination of state and international securities regulations.

Federal Registration of Investment Advisers

Any person who falls within the federal definition of "investment adviser" must register with the SEC under the Investment Advisers Act of 1940, which was amended by the NSMIA. SEC-registered investment advisers are known as *federally registered* investment advisers.

The following advisers must register with the SEC:

- persons managing $25 million or more in assets
- investment company advisers
- advisers not regulated under state law

An investment adviser that is not subject to federal registration requirements must register with the state in which it conducts business. For example, an investment adviser managing less than $25 million in assets must register with the state.

Federally registered investment advisers are exempt from state registration. While exempt from state registration, these investment advisers are still required to pay state filing fees and give notice.

State administrators are responsible for overseeing the business activities of all investment advisers that conduct business *within* the state and for enforcing the antifraud provisions under state and federal law.

Exemptions from Federal Registration

If an investment adviser meets one of the following conditions, he is exempt from the federal registration requirements of the Investment Advisers Act of 1940.

Local (intrastate) adviser exemption. The act of 1940 exempts from registration an investment adviser whose only clients are residents of the state in which the adviser is located and who does not give investment advice regarding securities that are listed, or admitted to unlisted trading privileges, on a national securities exchange.

De minimis exemption. Federal law also exempts a person whose investment advisory business is so small that the law considers it not worth regulating. (The term "de minimis" comes from a Latin phrase that means "the law does not concern itself with small things.") This exemption includes any investment adviser who has less than *15 clients* during the preceding 12 months and who does not hold himself out generally to the public as an investment adviser.

Insurance company advisory exemption. Exempt from registration under the act of 1940 are investment advisers whose only clients are insurance companies.

Burden of proof of exemption. The burden of proving an exemption from registration lies with the person claiming the exemption.

Federal registration of investment adviser representatives. A federally registered investment adviser must file information about its representatives (also called *supervised persons*) with the SEC. However, investment adviser representatives need not be registered individually with the SEC.

State Registration of Investment Advisers

The Uniform Securities Act (USA) is the model state law that governs the registration and regulation of investment advisers at the state level. Many, although not all, of the provisions of the Investment Advisers Act of 1940 have been adopted by the *North American Securities Administrators Association* **(NASAA)**, the trade organization for state securities administrators of the United States, Canada and Mexico. Under the USA, it is unlawful for *any* person to transact business in a state as an investment adviser or representative unless the person is registered with the state or exempt from registration. Investment advisers are exempt from state registration if they manage registered investment company portfolios or portfolios with $25 million or more in assets.

Exemptions from State Registration

Both the Investment Advisers Act of 1940 and the USA exempt from state registration any investment adviser that does minimal business in the state. This is known as the national *de minimis* exemption. The federal government also mandates a de minimis exemption from state registration. Under a provision of the National Securities Markets Improvement Act, a state may not require registration of an investment adviser if the adviser has directed business communications to fewer than six clients in the past 12-month period.

An exemption under the USA is also available to a person who has no place of business in the state and who limits his clientele to:

- other investment advisers;
- broker-dealers; and
- financial or institutional investors (such as banks, insurance companies or investment companies).

State registration of investment adviser representatives (supervised persons). An investment adviser representative who has a place of business in the state must register with the state. However, if the representative is a supervised person of a federally registered investment adviser, he is typically exempt from state registration, though, he must still pay filing fees. Under the USA, an individual need not register as an investment adviser representative if he acts in a clerical or an administrative capacity for the investment adviser.

State Registration Procedure

Application. An investment adviser or investment adviser rep may obtain an initial registration by filing (1) an application (Form ADV) with (2) the appropriate filing fee (as set by each state) and (3) a consent to service of process with the administrator (in the form the administrator requires).

A consent to service of process gives the administrator the irrevocable right to receive and process, as the applicant's attorney, any legal complaints that may arise in regard to an applicant's conduct as an investment adviser or an investment adviser rep. Once the applicant files the consent to service of process, any complaint presented to the administrator has the same force and validity as if it had been served personally on the applicant.

In addition to Form ADV, the adviser must file a balance sheet for the last fiscal year. If applicable, an investment adviser must furnish a copy of his surety bond and documentation that the appropriate licensing requirements were met.

The administrator may also require an applicant for initial registration to publish an announcement of the registration application in one or more specific newspapers in the state.

If the administrator does not deny the registration or is not in the process of denying the registration, that registration becomes effective at noon of the 30th day after the application is filed. The administrator may allow an earlier effective date. He also may defer the effective date until noon of the 30th day after the filing of any amendment.

Financial requirements. Under the USA, the state administrator may require, as a condition of registration, that an investment adviser meet minimum financial requirements. An investment adviser that has custody of customer assets must maintain a minimum net worth (assets minus liabilities) of $35,000. An investment adviser that has discretionary authority over customer accounts but that does not have custody must maintain a minimum net worth of $10,000.

Surety bonds. Investment advisers may be required by the administrator to post **surety bonds** if the person has custody of or discretionary authority over customer funds or securities. Typically, surety bonds are set in amounts of $35,000, although deposits of cash or securities may be permissible instead of the bonds. Compliance with minimum financial requirements releases the investment adviser from the surety bond requirement.

Registration Regulations and Restrictions

Qualification examinations. The administrator may require that one or more officers or representatives of an investment advisory firm take an examination that may be written, oral or both.

Successful completion of the Uniform Securities Agent State Law Examination (Series 63), the Uniform Investment Adviser Law Examination (Series 65), the Uniform Combined State Law Examination (Series 66) or any of the National Association of Securities Dealers (NASD), New York Stock Exchange (NYSE) or Municipal Securities Rulemaking Board (MSRB) examinations does not automatically constitute registration in a state. An applicant who has passed the exam does not have the right to transact business until the state administrator grants him registration.

Responsibilities of those who pass the examination. Successful completion of the Uniform Securities Agent State Law Examination does not relieve the agent of the following responsibilities:

- to know and abide by the specific requirements of the securities laws and the requirements of regulations of the states in which he will transact business;
- to understand that he does not have the right to transact business prior to being granted a license or registration; and
- to know that some states may require further certification to indicate that he has reviewed a state's blue-sky law and understands his responsibilities.

Denial, Suspension or Revocation of Registration

All registrations required by the Uniform Securities Act fall under the state administrators' jurisdiction. An administrator may deny, suspend or revoke any registration, or bar or censure any registrant, or restrict or limit any registrant's functions or activities if he finds that the:

- order is in the *public interest*; and
- the applicant, registrant or issuer of a security is guilty of any of a specified list of offenses.

Among these offenses are the following:

- filing of an incomplete, false or misleading application;
- willful violation of any Uniform Securities Act provision;
- conviction of a securities-related misdemeanor or felony within the past 10 years;
- permanent or temporary enjoinment (or injunction) by a court from investment-related activities;
- violation of any federal or state securities or commodities law within the past 10 years;
- engagement in dishonest or unethical securities practices;
- insolvency;
- willful violation of a foreign jurisdiction's securities or banking laws;
- denial, revocation or suspension of license by a foreign securities regulatory authority within the past five years;
- lack of qualification on the basis of training, experience or knowledge;
- failure to supervise registered employees; or
- failure to pay application filing fees.

Denial of registration due to lack of qualification. An individual's registration may be denied, revoked or suspended due to deficiencies in knowledge, training or experience. The administrator may not, however, deny registration solely on the lack of experience. Likewise, an investment adviser may not be denied licensing privileges based solely on the lack of its reps' experience.

The act authorizes the administrator to restrict a particular applicant's registration to that of a broker-dealer if the administrator finds the individual is not qualified as an investment adviser. Experience is a consideration, but lack of experience cannot be the sole factor for denying registration.

A representative need not meet the same level of qualification as the broker-dealer or investment adviser for which he works. A person registered and with experience as a broker-dealer or an agent is not necessarily qualified to be registered as an investment adviser. The broker-dealer may be prohibited from transacting business in any state as an investment adviser until such time as it does become registered.

Legal action. The Uniform Securities Act authorizes an administrator to proceed with legal action against an entire investment advisory firm if any one of that firm's officers has been disqualified, as long as this legal action is in the public interest. However, disqualification of an investment adviser rep, sometimes known as a *counselor*, may not be used automatically as a basis for taking legal action against the rep's entire firm unless further findings show that the firm's illegal actions (improper supervision, for example) were responsible for the rep's disqualification.

Withdrawal from registration. If a person or firm withdraws from registration, that withdrawal normally becomes effective 30 days after the administrator receives it, although the administrator may specify a shorter period of time if he so chooses. If a proceeding to revoke, deny or suspend the registration has begun, the effective date of the withdrawal will be delayed until whatever date the administrator determines is necessary to finalize the matter under consideration.

Notification requirements. The administrator must provide to any persons affected by an order under this section (1) advance notice of actions to deny, suspend or revoke registration to the persons affected and to the employer or prospective employer, (2) an opportunity for a hearing within 15 days of a written request and (3) a *written* statement of any findings, facts or conclusions.

Judicial review. A person who wishes to appeal the state administrator's decision or order may file a written petition in court within 60 days of the effective date of the order. The court may then decide whether to affirm or set aside the administrator's order.

Cancelation of Registration

An administrator may cancel any applicant's registration if he finds the applicant:

- is no longer in existence or has ceased to do business as an investment adviser;
- has been adjudged mentally incompetent or has been placed under the control of a guardian or conservator; or
- cannot be found after a reasonable search.

Federal and State Laws Regarding Investment Advisers

Table 2.1 compares federal and state registration requirements for investment advisers.

Table 2.2 on the following page compares federal laws and regulations to state laws under the Uniform Securities Act.

Forms Filed by Investment Advisers

Table 2.3 lists the forms that investment advisers must file and the purpose of each form.

Table 2.1   Summary of Revised Registration Requirements for Investment Advisers

Federally Registered	*State Registered*
Manage $25 million or more	Manage less than $25 million
State registration not required	Federal registration not required
Payment of federal and state filing fees required	Payment of state filing fee required
Federal registration of investment adviser reps not required; state registration may be required	State registration of investment adviser reps required

Table 2.3   Forms Investment Advisers File

Form	*Purpose*
ADV (Parts I and II)	Application for initial registration
ADV-E	Record of customer assets held in custody
ADV-W	Withdrawal of registration
Schedule H	Disclosure of wrap fee program

Table 2.2   Comparison of Federal and State Laws Regarding Investment Advisers

Item	Federal Law	State Law
Definition of "Investment Adviser" (IA)	Anyone who, for a fee, is "in the business of" advising others as to the worth of securities and who makes specific recommendations as part of his regular course of business, including issuing analyses and reports.	Same.
Exclusions	Bank; lawyer; accountant; engineer; teacher; broker-dealer; publisher of general news magazine; anyone whose advice is limited to U.S. government bonds.	Bank; lawyer; accountant; engineer; teacher; broker-dealer; publisher of general news magazine; IA representative.
Exemptions	All clients are residents of the adviser's state and no advice is rendered regarding exchange-listed securities; or all clients are insurance companies.	No place of business within the state and the only clients are institutions (investment companies, banks and insurance companies), broker-dealers, other IAs, employee benefit plans of $1 million or more, or government agencies.
	De minimis: Has had fewer than 15 clients (none of which are investment companies) during the previous 12 months and does not hold himself out to the public as an IA.	National de minimis: Has directed communications to fewer than six clients who are residents of the state during the previous 12 months.
Registration	File Form ADV with the SEC; effective within 45 days. No net capital requirement. No surety bonds. File for withdrawal on ADV-W.	File Form ADV with the administrator; effective at 12:00 pm on the 30th day. Net worth or surety bond required when IA has custody or discretion.
Criminal Penalties	Five years in jail and a $10,000 fine.	Three years in jail and a $5,000 fine.
Records	Must be readily accessible for 5 years; must be in the IA's main office for 2 of the years.	Same.
Assignment of Contract	Contract may not be assigned without the client's consent.	Same.
Change in Partnership Membership	The IA must notify the client of any change in partnership membership.	Same.
"Brochure Rule"	The "Brochure Rule" applies.	Same.
Use of Terms	The term "investment counsel" may not be used *unless:* the principal business is investment advice *and* a substantial portion is providing investment supervisory services (i.e., giving continuous advice on the investment of funds based on clients' individual needs).	An investment adviser representative is an associated person (not a clerk) of an adviser firm who makes recommendations; manages accounts; solicits advisory services; or supervises any of these activities.
Withdrawal of Registration	Takes effect 60 days after filing Form ADV-W.	Takes effect 30 days after filing Form ADV-W.
Insolvency	Not a cause for revocation.	Cause for revocation.

Business Activities of Investment Advisers

Investment Adviser Brochure Rule

Both federally registered and state-registered investment advisers must send a **written disclosure statement**, also known as a **disclosure brochure**, to each client.

Delivery. The adviser must deliver this brochure (1) *not less than 48 hours* before entering into a contract with a new client or (2) at the time of entering into the advisory contract *provided* the contract stipulates that the client has the right to terminate the agreement without penalty within five business days of signing the contract. The adviser must also send, or offer to send, each client a copy of the disclosure brochure at least annually (or more often if it has been changed or amended) at no cost or obligation to the client. If a client makes a written request for a copy of the brochure, it must be delivered or mailed within seven days of receipt of the request.

Contents. The brochure that the investment adviser delivers must contain substantially the same information as is required on Part II of **Form ADV** (and may, if the adviser wishes, be a copy of Part II). A copy of Form ADV Part II is reproduced in the Appendix, pages 155 through 162. Form ADV is intended to provide investment advisory clients with information about the investment adviser and his advisory business. It includes such facts as:

- name and address of the investment adviser or the organization;
- nature of the business, including the manner in which advice will be given (for example, issuing periodicals, consulting or producing charts and graphs);
- advisory services and fees;
- types of clients;
- types of investments;
- methods of analysis, sources of information and investment strategies;
- education, business standards and business background of the adviser;
- other business activities of the adviser;
- other financial industry activities or affiliations;
- participation or interest in client transactions;
- conditions for managing accounts;
- review of accounts;
- investment or brokerage discretion;
- additional compensation; and
- balance sheet.

Exceptions. Two principal exceptions to the brochure delivery rule exist. The adviser need not deliver a brochure if the advisory client is (1) an investment company or (2) contracting for impersonal advisory services requiring a payment of less than $200.

Wrap Fee Brochure

Definition. According to the USA and the 1940 act, a wrap fee program is an arrangement under which the investment adviser, also called the *sponsor,* receives a flat fee for providing investment advisory services and executing client transactions. Investment advisory services may include recommending securities or recommending other investment advisers. The compensation the adviser receives under a wrap fee program is not directly related to the transactions executed for the client's account.

Disclosure. Information about an adviser's wrap fee program is filed with the regulators on Schedule H of Form ADV. At a minimum, the sponsor must provide to wrap fee clients a wrap fee brochure that contains the same information contained in the investment adviser brochure. If the sponsor provides further information regarding wrap fee programs, it must be specific to the program being offered to a client. The wrap fee brochure is subject to the same delivery requirements as the investment adviser brochure.

Sales and Advertising Materials

The administrator may require a state-registered investment adviser to file any informational materials or advertisements that are distributed to clients or prospective clients unless the security or transaction is exempted under the act. It is unlawful for any person subject to the act to file any misleading or fraudulent material.

Recordkeeping and Reporting Requirements

Both federally registered and state-registered investment advisers must keep and maintain any records, accounts, correspondences or papers as required. The state administrator or the SEC has the authority to examine all of an investment adviser's records at any time and place, without advance notice. These examinations may take the form of audits by the SEC or the state's administrator. These audits can be conducted in any state, as the administrator deems necessary or appropriate.

The records may be kept in any normally acceptable manner, including photographic (microfilm) and computer (disk) formats, as long as there exists the means to access (read) and make copies of the records as needed.

The USA and the 1940 act set requirements for investment adviser recordkeeping. The following records must be kept in an easily accessible place for five years (for the first two years, they must be kept in an office of the investment adviser):

- journals and other records of original entry;
- ledgers of assets, liabilities, reserves, capital, and income and expense accounts;
- order memorandums showing the following:
  - terms, conditions and special instructions of the order
  - identity of the person who recommended the transaction

- account
- date of entry
- bank, broker or other party through whom the order was executed
- whether discretionary power was exercised
- check books, bank statements, canceled checks and cash reconciliations;
- trial balances, financial statements and internal audit working papers;
- originals of all written communications received and copies of all written communications sent by the adviser relating to recommendations (if the advisory communication was sent to more than 10 persons, their names and addresses also must be recorded), receipts and disbursements of funds, and the placing of orders;
- list of accounts over which the adviser has discretionary power and copies of the powers of attorney for those accounts;
- written agreements between the adviser and each client;
- record of any transaction in which the adviser has a beneficial (ownership) or control interest;
- copies of written statements sent to clients;
- written acknowledgments from clients that they have received the required disclosure documents; and
- copies of any working papers relating to the calculation of performance or rates of return.

Advisers with custody of customer funds and securities. In addition to the records listed, an adviser who has custody of customer funds or securities must keep, and post at least daily, the following records:

- journal showing all purchases, receipts and deliveries of securities and cash;
- separate ledger for each customer showing all purchases, sales receipts and deliveries of securities, with dates and prices;
- copies of all confirmations; and
- securities records showing the names of clients who have positions in those securities.

Institutional investment managers who exercise discretion over accounts valued at more than $100 million must file quarterly and annual statements on Form 13F.

Business-related records. Under the act of 1940, partnership records, articles of incorporation, charters, minute books and other records relating to the investment adviser's business enterprise must be kept for three years after the termination of the business. It is the adviser's responsibility to make arrangements for the retention of these records after the firm ceases to do business, and he must inform the SEC in writing of these arrangements.

Advisers who operate investment supervisory or management services.
If an investment adviser offers investment supervisory or management services, he must keep separate records for each client showing the securities purchased and sold, including the date, amount and price, and must be able to list clients' names by security position.

Financial Reports

Every registered broker-dealer and investment adviser must file all financial reports—including balance sheets, income statements, FOCUS reports and net capital reports—that the SEC or the administrator prescribes. The reports must be filed within 90 days of the end of the firm's fiscal year.

Prepayment of fees. If an investment adviser requires clients to pay fees exceeding $500 per client six months or more in advance, the adviser must file an audited balance sheet as of the end of the adviser's fiscal year.

Amendments to Records

If the information contained in any document filed with the SEC, the appropriate SRO (for example, the NASD) or the administrator is or becomes inaccurate or incomplete in any material respect, the registrant must file a correcting amendment promptly.

Custody of Customer Funds and Securities

The administrator may prohibit state-registered investment advisers from taking custody of customer assets. If custody is not prohibited, an investment adviser must notify the administrator if the adviser has or may have custody.

The Uniform Securities Act and the Investment Advisers Act of 1940 set out similar guidelines for the handling of customer funds and securities. Whether registered with the state or with the SEC, an investment adviser who has custody of customer funds and securities must ensure that the funds and securities are segregated and are marked to identify the owners. If the customer funds and securities are to be deposited in a bank, the bank accounts must contain only customer funds and must identify the investment adviser who acts as agent for the customers. The investment adviser must keep complete and accurate records of all such deposits and accounts on Form ADV-E. An independent public accountant must verify the accounts at least once each year without prior notice to the adviser.

Customers who have funds or securities in an investment adviser's possession must be sent at least once every three months an itemized statement showing these funds and securities as well as all transactions, debits and credits that have occurred or exist in an account.

Investment Advisory Contracts

The typical investment adviser's business is based largely on contracts between the adviser and potential clients for advisory services for which the adviser will receive compensation. Both federally registered advisers and state-registered advisers are subject to regulations governing the form and content of many parts of these contracts, including those regulations outlining the methods of compensation, methods of consent and notification of changes.

Contract terms. Before entering into, extending or renewing an investment advisory contract, the investment adviser must ensure that the following terms are written into the contract:

- services to be provided;
- contract duration;
- advisory fee;
- formula for computing the advisory fee;
- amount of any prepaid fee to be returned in the event of contract termination;
- whether the investment adviser has been granted discretionary power; and
- the fact that assignment of the contract by the investment adviser can occur only with the party's consent to the contract.

Compensation restrictions. An investment adviser is prohibited from entering into any contract that bases compensation on a share of the capital gains or capital appreciation (or any other measure of performance) that the client or the account achieves. This prohibition includes:

- waiving or refunding the client's advisory fee if the account underperforms (contingent fees);
- engaging in any form of profit-sharing arrangement; and
- rebating commissions on mutual fund sales.

An investment adviser is permitted to enter into a contract with an investment company or an account with *net assets* of more than $1 million basing compensation on a percentage of net assets as long as the compensation is:

- based on the fund's or account's average value over a specified time period; and
- proportional to the fund's or account's performance compared to a standard performance benchmark or an index.

An investment adviser may receive reimbursement for reasonable expenses related to handling customer accounts.

Conditional exemption. An investment adviser may enter into a contract with a client that provides for performance-based compensation if *all* of the following conditions are met:

- the client may be a **qualified purchasers pool** (private investment companies);
- the client is not an investment company;
- the client is an individual or a corporation with at least $500,000 under the investment adviser's management or is an individual with a net worth of at least $1 million;
- the formula by which the adviser's compensation is calculated (1) includes realized capital losses and unrealized depreciation and (2) bases the compensation on gains less losses for a period of not less than one year;
- certain disclosures are made before entering into the contract, including (1) that the performance compensation may create an incentive for the adviser to take greater risks, (2) that the compensation is based on realized as well as unrealized gains, (3) the periods that will be used, (4) the nature

of any index used as a comparative measure and (5) how any securities for which no readily available market quotations exist will be valued; and

- the investment adviser reasonably believes that an arm's-length arrangement has been made and that the client understands the basis for the compensation.

Transactions

Discretionary Account Transactions

An adviser may direct transactions for a discretionary account to any broker-dealer, as long as the charges for services performed are reasonable and are disclosed in the client brochure. Clients must provide written permission before the adviser handles transactions on a discretionary basis.

Agency Cross Transactions

Definition. According to the USA and the 1940 act, an agency cross transaction is a transaction in which the investment adviser arranges a trade, acting either as agent or principal, on behalf of both the advisory client and the party on the other side of the transaction. For a state-registered investment adviser to effect an agency cross transaction, the adviser must also be registered as a broker-dealer in the state. For a federally registered investment adviser to effect an agency cross transaction, the person may be registered as an investment adviser or as a broker-dealer.

Conditions. An investment adviser may make an agency cross transaction if:

- the investment adviser has provided disclosure in advance that an agency cross transaction provides commissions to the adviser from both parties and thus causes a potential conflict of interest;
- after receiving the disclosure, the client gives written consent to such transactions;
- the adviser provides the client with a confirmation at or before the transaction's completion, stating the details of the transaction, the date and the source and amount of compensation the adviser received;
- the customer's account statements summarize the total number of agency cross transactions effected during the preceding period and the total amount of commissions received; and
- the client is notified that the written consent may be revoked at any time.

Restrictions. An investment adviser may not effect an agency cross transaction if the adviser has recommended the transaction to both the buyer and the seller. An adviser executing an agency cross transaction is still obligated to provide the best executions to his clients and must disclose whether he is acting as an agent or as a principal.

Advertisements by Investment Advisers

In general, every communication from an investment adviser to the public must be based on principles of fair dealing and good faith. Such communication should provide a sound basis for evaluating the facts in regard to the product, service or industry promoted. Exaggerated, unwarranted or misleading statements or claims are strictly prohibited.

The definition of "advertisement" includes any notice, circular, letter or other written communication addressed to more than one person, or any other announcement (whether in a publication, over the radio, on television or through another medium) that offers any report, chart, formula or other service to be used in making investment decisions.

To guide advisers in creating and producing advertising and sales literature, the following specific requirements apply.

Identification. In general, sales literature must identify the following:

- name of the member firm;
- person or firm that prepared the material if copy was prepared outside;
- date the material was first used; and
- whether any price or market performance data or other pertinent information cited in the literature is not current.

Using past stock selection records. It is acceptable to use lists of stock and other security recommendations the investment adviser made in the past provided that the following conditions are met:

- The list of recommendations and any accompanying text must not imply that comparable future performance can be expected.
- The list must include all recommendations made (gainers and losers) over the selected period of time (at least the previous one year).

Claims and opinions couched as facts and conclusions. It is both unprofessional and a violation of the regulations to pass off opinions, projections, charts, graphics, formulas and forecasts as guarantees of performance or as scientific evidence.

Testimonials. The use by celebrities and influencers of public opinion of testimonials and endorsements related to specific recommendations, results, advice, analyses, reports or other services is strictly prohibited. This prohibition does not, however, prevent an investment adviser from hiring a well-known spokesperson for an advertisement or a campaign, as long as that person does not imply that she uses the investment adviser's services.

Offers of free service. It is unprofessional to offer free services or free investment reports and topical news if, in fact, the respondent must assume obligations of some sort. Reports, analyses or other services offered to the public as "free" must be furnished entirely without condition or obligation.

Other Communication Prohibitions

The following lists other unprofessional practices as they relate to investment adviser advertisements:

- stating or implying that research facilities are more extensive than they actually are;
- using hedge clauses, caveats and disclaimers if they are misleading or inconsistent with the content of the material;
- making ambiguous references to the SEC, an SRO or another organization, with the aim of leading people to believe that the adviser acts with the sponsorship, recommendation, endorsement or approval of the SEC, SRO or other organization, or that any of these has passed on the adviser's merits or qualifications;
- using the initials "RIA" after the adviser's name with the aim of implying he has attained a certain level of education or qualification (the description "registered investment adviser" may be used); and
- in the case of advertisements or sales literature that includes price performance information in the form of charts, graphs or statistical tables prepared by or obtained from outside sources, not disclosing the source of the data used.

Disclosure of Financial and Disciplinary Information

Both state-registered advisers and federally registered advisers must disclose to clients any financial information that could have an impact on the type or quality of the advisory services offered. They are also required to disclose any legal or disciplinary actions—including civil, criminal and SRO—against them that could have a bearing on a client's capability to evaluate an adviser's integrity or ability to meet contractual commitments.

SEC Release IA-1092

Persons Considered Investment Advisers

SEC Release IA-1092 was issued to clarify the application of the Investment Advisers Act of 1940 to persons who provide investment advice as part of other financial services. The SEC and NASAA developed Release IA-1092 to provide uniform interpretation and application of federal and state advisers laws, as well as to define "in the business" with respect to investment advisers. The release identifies the following three groups that are included in the act's definition of "investment adviser":

- financial planner who gives financial advice to individuals or families based on their needs and objectives (the advice might include general or specific recommendations as to insurance, savings, investments, retirement, taxes or estate planning);

- pension consultant who offers administrative services to employee benefit plans and their fiduciaries, and who may also offer general or specific advisory services; and

- sports or entertainment representative who manages the career of an athlete or entertainer. The representative may negotiate contracts, organize promotions and provide tax planning and money management services and often has discretion over the client's money (for example, the representative may pay the client's bills).

Investment Adviser Status

Release IA-1092 discusses the 1940 act's three tests for determining whether a person is an investment adviser. All three tests must be met to fit the definition of "investment adviser."

Advice or analyses concerning securities. A person who limits advice to general categories of investments without recommending securities by name is considered an investment adviser. This includes a person who provides a comparison of securities with insurance or other nonsecurities products.

The "business standard." The degree of advisory activities determines whether a person is "in the business of" providing investment advice. If the person holds herself out to the public as an adviser, receives separate compensation for advice or gives advice on anything other than rare and isolated occasions, she meets the requirements of this test. A person who makes a simple recommendation that a client diversify his assets is not considered to be in the business of giving investment advice.

Compensation. A person who receives any economic benefit as a result of providing investment advice is considered an investment adviser. This includes compensation received from insurance-based products. The compensation may be direct or indirect; for example, the adviser may receive a fee from the firm executing the recommended transaction rather than from the client.

Disclosing Conflicts of Interest

The antifraud provisions of the Investment Advisers Act of 1940 require advisers to disclose material facts, especially those concerning a conflict of interest. SEC Release IA-1092 includes the following illustrations of such disclosures:

- If an adviser is associated with a broker-dealer or an insurance company through which the adviser's plans will be implemented, the adviser must disclose that she is acting as an agent for the broker-dealer or insurance company.

- If a registered representative provides investment advice outside of the scope of his employment with a broker-dealer, the rep must disclose that he is making recommendations independently from the firm.
- If an investment adviser recommends that a client execute transactions through a broker-dealer associated with the adviser, the adviser must also inform the client that the transactions may be executed by another broker-dealer.
- If an investment adviser recommends only those products available through a broker-dealer associated with the adviser, the adviser must disclose that the recommendations are limited.
- If at any time an adviser's personal interests conflict with a client's, he must disclose that his personal transactions are inconsistent with the recommendations he's given to the client.

Enforcement of the Investment Advisers Act of 1940

Both the state administrator and the SEC are required to enforce antifraud provisions for all investment advisers, whether the advisers are federally registered or state-registered.

SEC enforcement. The SEC reserves the right to enforce the provisions of the act of 1940 either upon receiving a complaint or if it appears to the SEC that a violation of the act has occurred or could occur. As part of its jurisdiction, the SEC has the right to require any federally registered investment adviser to file with it a written, sworn statement covering all of the relevant facts and circumstances relating to the incident(s). The SEC has the right to fully investigate the incident, including the circumstances surrounding or contributing to it and any persons involved.

In exercising its enforcement rights, the SEC may bring an action in a district court against a person believed to be (or about to be) in violation of the act, and a restraining order or temporary injunction may be granted.

Civil penalties. If it appears to the SEC that a person has violated a rule under the act of 1940, it may seek civil penalties against that person. A violation can be placed into one of three "tiers." Depending on how the violation is classified, the penalty can range up to $100,000 for a natural person (individual), $500,000 for any other person, or the amount of the gain that resulted from the violation (for a third-tier violation). SEC-imposed penalties are payable directly to the U.S. Treasury.

Criminal penalties. If the violation cannot be classified into the three-tier system, the SEC can impose a criminal penalty of up to $10,000, imprisonment for not more than five years, or both. (The Uniform Securities Act allows for a maximum fine of $5,000, imprisonment for not more than three years, or both.) The SEC or state administrator will refer the case to the criminal courts if there is evidence of criminal activity.

Availability of Information

Public access to investment adviser registration form. Information filed by an investment adviser in a registration form is considered public domain information and, as such, is available to the public on request (and on payment of a reasonable charge to cover the costs of search, photocopies and so on).

Confidentiality of investigations. If an investigation, an examination or a similar action is under way at the time of a request for information, this fact and any information produced by the investigation need not be disclosed to anyone who is not an SEC member, officer or employee.

Enforcement of the Uniform Securities Act

A state administrator has full jurisdiction over *only* those investment advisers registered with the state. The administrator enforces the USA provisions with regard to state-registered investment advisers. However, the state administrator is also required to enforce all antifraud provisions as they pertain to *any* adviser that conducts business in the state.

3 ◇ Regulation of New Issues

Key Terms

advertising prospectus
cooling-off period
covered security
Glass-Steagall Act of 1933
indication of interest
initial public offering (IPO)
investment banker
new issue market
omitting prospectus
preliminary prospectus
primary offering

private placement
red herring
registration statement
secondary offering
Securities Act of 1933
Securities Exchange Act of 1934
shelf offering
split offering
tombstone
Trust Indenture Act of 1939
underwriting

Overview

Securities industry legislation at both the federal and the state levels is designed to protect investors by requiring proper disclosure of information and establishing procedures that safeguard against fraud and misrepresentation. Securities laws at the state level are known as *blue-sky laws;* they deal with issues such as the state registration requirements for securities, broker-dealers, investment advisers and representatives. The Uniform Securities Act is model legislation that most states have adopted or have adapted to meet specific state requirements.

This chapter also describes the major pieces of federal securities legislation: the Securities Act of 1933 and the Securities Exchange Act of 1934, with the subsequent acts that expanded or amended these basic regulations.

Overview of New Issue Regulation

The Crash of 1929

During the early 1900s, America enjoyed a long-term bull market that promised to last forever. Attracted by the dream of easy money, Americans turned en masse to Wall Street, poring over stock price tables and learning the language of trading operations. For the first time, the general public became a significant factor in the market; but often they purchased securities knowing little or nothing about the issuing companies or their plans for spending the money.

Investors borrowed heavily; that is, they bought securities *on margin*. Doing so was an act of faith in the perpetual bull market and an outcome of generous credit policies that allowed investors to borrow most of the purchase price of stock. By the summer of 1929, more than a million Americans held stock on margin.

The rest is familiar history. Stock prices reached new heights in early September 1929. Then things fell apart. By the third week of September, tumbling prices brought the Dow Jones averages down 19 points. A month later, averages were 50 points below the September high mark. The downward spiral of prices gained momentum, breaking through crumbling layers of anticipated buying support.

Rapidly declining prices meant investors' stocks were no longer adequate security for the loans they had taken out to buy them. Securities purchased on very low margins, therefore, were sold to raise money, and this caused even deeper drops in market prices. Stock dumping destroyed grassroots investors and wealthy traders alike, including those supposedly safe investment trusts, which unloaded their holdings for whatever they could bring.

The Legislative Reaction

After the crash, the market continued to decline for several years. During that time, Congress examined the causes of the debacle and passed several laws meant to prevent its recurrence. This legislation included, among other acts, the Securities Act of 1933, the Glass-Steagall Act of 1933 and the Securities Exchange Act of 1934.

The Securities Act of 1933. The Securities Act of 1933 requires securities issuers to provide sufficient information for investors to make fully informed buying decisions. This information must be registered with the federal government and published in a prospectus. The act outlaws fraud committed in connection with the underwriting and issuing of all securities, including exempt securities.

The Glass-Steagall Act (Banking Act) of 1933. Securities firms were not the only financial companies to go belly-up in the early 1930s. Banks, too, went broke in vast numbers. Congress concluded that one factor in the general financial collapse was the fact that commercial bankers engaged in investment banking. In their role as commercial bankers, they took deposits and financed commercial enterprises. As investment bankers, they underwrote stocks, using deposits to finance their securities ventures. Losses on a bank's investment side, therefore, affected the health of its commercial operations.

With the Glass-Steagall Act, Congress attempted to erect a wall between commercial banking and investment banking. The act forbids commercial banks to underwrite securities (except municipal general obligation bonds) and denies investment bankers the right to open deposit accounts or make commercial loans.

The Securities Exchange Act of 1934. The Securities Exchange Act of 1934 addresses secondary trading of securities, personnel involved in secondary trading and fraudulent trading practices. It also created the Securities and Exchange Commission (SEC), a government agency, to oversee the industry.

In 1938, the act was broadened when it was amended by the **Maloney Act**, which provides for the establishment of a self-regulatory body to help police the industry. Under the provisions of the Maloney Act, the National Association of Securities Dealers (NASD) regulates over-the-counter (OTC) trading in much the same way as the exchanges regulate their members.

The Trust Indenture Act of 1939. The Trust Indenture Act of 1939 was created, in part, to provide the same sort of protection to the purchasers of debt securities as investors in equities receive. The term "debt securities" includes all notes, bonds, debentures and other similar evidences of indebtedness. The term "trust indenture" covers any mortgage, trust or other indenture, or any similar instrument or agreement.

As its major focus and means of protecting the public interest, the act prohibits the sale of any corporate debt security unless it has been issued under a **trust indenture**. In addition to full disclosure about the nature of the debt issue and the issuer, the trust indenture identifies the trustee's responsibilities, rights and powers.

The trust indenture is the contract that gives the appointed trustee the powers necessary to enforce the issuer's obligations and the debt holders' rights. Among the trustee's responsibilities is to represent future investors in the indenture's preparation.

Federal Registration of New Issues

The Legislation

The Securities Act of 1933 regulates new issues of corporate securities sold to the public. The act also is referred to as the *Full Disclosure Act*, the *New Issues Act*, the *Truth in Securities Act* and the *Prospectus Act*. It requires the registration of new issues (debt and equity) before they may be sold to the public. The main purpose of the act is to ensure that the investing public is fully informed about a security and its issuing company when the security is first sold to the public. The act requires registration of new issues of nonexempt securities with the SEC. It also requires that a **prospectus** (a written offer to sell a security), which contains information derived from the registration statement, be given to buyers.

The 1933 act protects the investor considering purchase of new issues by:

- requiring registration of new issues that are to be distributed interstate;
- requiring each issuer to provide full and fair disclosure about itself and the offering;
- requiring each issuer to make available all material information necessary for the investor to judge the issue's merit;
- regulating the underwriting and distribution of primary and secondary issues; and
- providing *criminal penalties* for fraud in the issuance of new securities.

When a corporation wants to issue its securities to the public, the SEC requires it to supply:

- detailed information about itself and its securities to the SEC; and
- the relevant portion of that information to the general investing public.

A **registration statement** disclosing material information must be filed with the SEC by the issuer. Part of the registration statement is a prospectus, which must be provided to all purchasers of the new issue. A prospectus contains much of the same information included in the registration statement, but without the supporting documentation. The registration statement must contain:

- a description of the issuer's business;
- the names and addresses of corporate officers and directors, their salaries and a five-year business history of each;
- the amount of corporate securities owned by these key people and by owners of 10 percent or more of the company;
- the company's capitalization, including its equity and amount of funded debt;
- a description of how the proceeds will be used; and
- whether the company is involved in any legal proceedings.

The Prospectus

The preliminary prospectus. After an issuer files a registration statement with the SEC, a **cooling-off** period begins. This period lasts 20 days, during which the SEC reviews a security's registration statement and can issue a **stop order** if the prospectus does not contain all of the required information. During the cooling-off period, a registered rep may discuss the new issue with clients and provide them with a **preliminary prospectus**, also known as a **red herring**. A registered rep *may not* send any other material to potential customers with the preliminary prospectus, including research reports, *Value Line* sheets, marketing letters and so on.

A red herring need not include the securities' final price, commissions, dealer discounts or net proceeds to the company, although pricing formulas and other information are often included. The document must carry a legend to the effect that a registration statement has been filed with the SEC, but is not yet effective. By law, this disclaimer message must be printed in red ink.

SEC rules prohibit the sale of public offering securities other than by prospectus, which means that no sales are allowed unless and until the buyer is furnished with a final prospectus; that is, securities may be *sold by prospectus only*.

However, the SEC does allow the use of preliminary prospectuses (essentially all the same information found in a final prospectus, but with only a POP range or no price at all) as prospecting tools. The underwriters and selling group members thus have a document to use as they test for investor receptivity and gather **indications of interest**.

An indication of interest is just that—a broker-dealer's or investor's declaration that it might be interested in purchasing some of the security from the underwriter after the security comes out of registration. An indication of interest is *not* a commitment to buy because sales are prohibited until after the registration becomes effective (the *effective date*).

The final prospectus. When the registration statement becomes effective, the issuer amends the preliminary prospectus and adds information, including the final offering price and the underwriting spread. This revised report becomes the final prospectus. Registered representatives may then take orders from those customers who indicated an interest in buying during the cooling-off period.

A copy of the final prospectus must precede or accompany all sales confirmations. The prospectus should include all of the following information:

- description of the offering
- price of the offering
- selling discounts
- date of the offering (effective date)
- use of the proceeds
- description of the underwriting, but not the actual contract
- statement of the possibility that the issue's price may be stabilized
- history of the business
- risks to the purchasers
- description of management
- material financial information
- legal opinion concerning the formation of the corporation
- SEC disclaimer

Advertising Prospectus

The National Securities Markets Improvement Act of 1996 includes an amendment to the 1940 act that allows an investment company to distribute an *advertising prospectus*. An advertising prospectus offers considerably more flexibility than other permitted forms of advertising. The advertising prospectus is not restricted to the information disclosed in the summary prospectus, and it may include historical performance data. Unlike the summary prospectus, the advertising prospectus need not be filed as part of the registration statement.

Financial Reports

The act of 1940 requires that shareholders receive financial reports at least semiannually (every six months). Under the NSMIA, the SEC may now require reports to be provided more frequently to keep the information reasonably current. Investment companies are no longer required to state reporting requirements. These reports must contain:

- the investment company's balance sheet;
- a valuation of all securities in the investment company's portfolio on the date of the balance sheet (a portfolio list);
- the investment company's income statement;
- a complete statement of all compensation paid to the board of directors and to the advisory board; and
- a statement of the total dollar amount of securities purchased and sold during the period.

It is the principal's responsibility to see that each of these reports is current and accurately reflects the state of the company at the end of the reporting period. In addition, the company must send a copy of its balance sheet to any shareholder who makes a written request for one at any time between semiannual reports.

The investment company must be audited at least annually and distribute an audited annual report to every investor once a year.

Advertising a New Issue

Advertising and sales literature, as defined by Rule 134, include any notice, circular, advertisement, letter or other communication published or transmitted to any person. The only advertising allowed during the cooling-off period is commonly referred to as a **tombstone (omitting prospectus)**, defined by SEC Rule 482; it is a simple statement of facts without embellishment. The tombstone announces a new issue, but does not offer the securities for sale (an offer for sale can be made only by prospectus) and is not distributed with an application form of any sort.

Advertising copy and other sales materials will qualify as tombstones and will not be deemed a prospectus—which means they need not be filed with the SEC as part of the registration statement—if the body copy is limited to the following:

- name of the issuer of the securities being offered (or the name of the person or company whose assets are to be sold in exchange for the securities being offered);
- brief description of the business of the person making the offer;
- date, time and place of the meeting at which stockholders are to vote on or consent to the proposed transaction (exchange of securities or sale of assets);
- brief description of the planned transaction (material facts and financial information); and/or
- any legend or disclaimer statement required by state or federal law.

Civil Liabilities under the Act of 1933

Untruths in Registration Statements

If a registration statement contains untrue statements of material fact or omits material facts, any person acquiring the security may sue any or all of the following:

- those who signed the registration statement;
- directors and partners of the issuer;
- anyone named in the registration statement as being or about to become a director or partner of the company;
- accountants, appraisers and other professionals who contributed to the registration statement; and
- the underwriters.

Statute of limitations. A civil lawsuit to recover damages incurred owing to untrue statements or omissions of material facts in a registration statement must be filed within three years after the sale of the security.

Untruths in Prospectuses and Communications

The seller of any security being sold by prospectus—which includes oral communications based on information contained in a security's prospectus—will be liable to the purchaser if the prospectus contains misstatements or omissions of material facts. For example, an issuer states in its prospectus that it has made consistent repayment of bond principal and interest to its bondholders. However, if in fact its outstanding bonds carry a rating that indicates a high risk of default, the issuer's prospectus contains a misstatement of this material fact. To avoid civil liability, the seller must prove that he did not know of the misstatements or omissions and that he exercised reasonable care at the time of the sale to prevent communicating any untrue or misleading information of a material nature.

Misrepresentations

It is unlawful for a seller to tell a purchaser of a security that the information contained in the registration statement (and, therefore, in the prospectus) must be 100 percent true and complete as evidenced by the fact that the SEC has not issued a stop order.

The Underwriting Process

Underwriting Corporate Securities

The first successful securities underwriting in the United States is attributed to Jay Cooke. During the Civil War, he and his force of bond salesmen placed more than $2 billion in U.S. government bonds with private investors throughout the North. By fostering these financial ties between government and investors, Cooke's sales force reinforced the loyalty and patriotism of many investors.

After the war ended, securities underwriting continued to be critical to the economic development of the United States. Today, publicly owned and financed corporations dominate U.S. business. Each year, the underwriting activities of investment bankers provide billions of dollars in new equity and debt financing.

Investment Banking

A business or branch of municipal government that plans to issue securities usually works with an **investment banker**, a securities broker-dealer that may also specialize in underwriting new issues by helping to bring securities to market and sell them to investors.

An investment banker's functions may include:

- advising corporations on the best ways to raise long-term capital
- raising capital for issuers by distributing new securities
- buying securities from an issuer and reselling them to the public
- distributing large blocks of stock to the public and to institutions

Participants in a Corporate New Issue

Securities and Exchange Commission. When a corporation issues new securities, the SEC is responsible for the following:

- reviewing the registration statement filed for the offering (accomplished during the cooling-off period between the filing date and the effective date);
- sending a deficiency letter to the issuer if the review uncovers problems, thus halting the review until deficiencies are corrected, at which point the cooling-off period continues; and
- declaring the registration statement effective—that is, releasing the securities for sale.

The issuer. The issuer is the party selling the securities to raise money. The issuer's duties may include:

- filing the registration statement with the SEC;
- filing a registration statement with the states in which it intends to sell securities (also known as *blue-skying the issue*); and
- negotiating the securities' price and the amount of the spread with the underwriter.

National Association of Securities Dealers. The NASD Committee on Corporate Financing reviews the underwriting spread to determine fairness and reasonableness of underwriting compensation.

The individual states. State securities laws, also called **blue-sky laws**, may require state registration of new issues, broker-dealers and registered reps. As mentioned above, registering securities with the state is called **blue-skying the issue**. The issuer or investment banker may blue-sky an issue by one of the following three methods:

- **Coordination**. The issuer registers simultaneously with the state and the SEC. Both registrations become effective on the same date.
- **Filing**. Certain states allow some new issues to blue-sky by having the issuers notify the state of registration with the SEC. In this case, no registration statement is required by the state, although certain other information must be filed.
- **Qualification**. The issue is registered with the state independent of federal registration, meeting all state requirements.

The underwriter. The underwriter not only assists with registration, but also may advise the corporate issuer on the best way to raise capital. The underwriter considers at least the following matters:

- **Whether to offer stock or bonds**. If stocks currently sell at depressed prices, bonds may seem the more attractive alternative. If bonds currently sell at high interest rates, the company may choose to issue stock.
- **Tax consequences of the offering**. The interest a corporation must pay on its bonds is tax deductible. The stock dividends it pays investors are paid out of aftertax profits.
- **Whether to go to the money market for short-term funds or to the capital market for long-term funds**. If the corporation decides to go to the capital market, it will issue one of the following types of securities: secured bonds, debentures, preferred stock or common stock.

Under the provisions of the Securities Act of 1933, offering such securities normally requires registration with the SEC unless a specific exemption applies.

Types of Offerings

Securities Markets

The **new issue market** consists of companies "going public"—privately owned businesses raising capital by selling common stock to the public for the first time. New issue securities are also known as **initial public offering (IPO)** securities.

The **additional issue market** is made up of new securities issues from companies that are already publicly owned; that is, they currently have stock outstanding with the public. These companies increase their equity capitalization by issuing more stock. This is accomplished when an underwriter either distributes the stock in a public offering or arranges for the shares to be sold in a private placement.

In addition to being classified by whether they represent initial or additional issues of new securities, offerings can be distinguished by the final distribution of their proceeds.

Primary Offering

In a primary offering, the underwriting proceeds go to the **issuing corporation**. The corporation increases its capitalization by selling stock, either a new issue or previously authorized but unissued stock. It may do this at any time and in any amount, provided the total stock outstanding never exceeds the amount authorized in the corporation's bylaws.

Secondary Offering

In a secondary offering, one or more major stockholders in the corporation sell all or a major portion of their holdings. The underwriting proceeds are paid to the stockholders rather than to the corporation itself. Typically, secondary offerings occur in situations where the founder of a business, and perhaps some of the original financial backers, determines that the company has more to gain by going public than by staying private.

Table 3.1 compares primary and secondary offerings.

Table 3.1   Offerings and Markets

	New Issue (IPO) Market	Additional Issue Market
Primary Offering	Company goes public; underwriting proceeds go to the company.	Company is already public; underwriting proceeds go to the company.
Secondary Offering	Company goes public; underwriting proceeds go to the selling stockholders.	Company is already public; underwriting proceeds go to the selling stockholders.

Split Offering (or Combined Distribution)

A split offering is a combination of a primary and a secondary offering. Some of the stock offered will be issued by the corporation, and the rest represents shares held by present corporate stockholders.

Shelf Offering (Rule 415)

Normally, an issuer sells all of the securities it has registered in a new issue as soon as it can. By doing so, the issuer brings in a large sum of money in a short amount of time. Faced with an immediate need for such a large sum, the issuer should not have a problem handling or investing the money. However, what if the issuer needs the same amount of cash, but in smaller portions over a year or two? A normal issue would provide all of the cash up front, but much of it would have to be invested elsewhere until the investor actually needed it. Delaying the issue could result in cash flow problems.

As an alternative, an issuer can register a new issue security without selling the entire issue at once through a **shelf offering**. The issuer can sell limited portions of a registered shelf offering over a two-year period without having to reregister the security or incurring penalties, but it must file a supplemental prospectus prior to each sale. Shelf offerings provide issuers and their investment bankers with flexibility—money can be raised and expenses incurred only as needed.

Exemptions from Federal Registration

Exempt Issuers and Securities

With certain exceptions, the Securities Act of 1933 requires the registration of new issues with the SEC. Certain securities are exempt from the registration statement and prospectus requirements of the 1933 act, either because of the issuer's creditworthiness or because another government regulatory agency has jurisdiction over the issuer. The following issuers and securities are not required to be registered with the SEC:

- U.S. government securities
- state and municipal bonds
- commercial paper and bankers' acceptances (maturities under 270 days)
- insurance policies and fixed annuity contracts (but not variable annuities)
- national and state bank securities (except bank holding companies)
- building and loan (S&L) securities
- common carrier (e.g., trucking, airline and railroad) securities
- farmers' cooperative securities
- small business investment company (SBIC) securities
- charitable, religious, educational and nonprofit association issues

Banks are exempted from SEC registration of securities because they file information on new issues with bank regulators, and that information is available to investors. This exemption applies only to the securities of banks, not to those of bank holding companies. Private transactions in securities are not covered by the 1933 and 1934 acts if they do not involve the use of the U.S. mail or other means of interstate commerce.

Insurance policies are not included in the definition of "security"; however, variable annuities, variable life insurance and variable universal life insurance are funded by *separate accounts* and must be registered as securities with the SEC.

Exempt Transactions

Even though neither the issuer nor the type of security is exempt, the manner of sale may qualify an offering for exemption. Securities offered by industrial, financial and other corporations may qualify for exemption from the registration statement and prospectus requirements of the 1933 act under one of the following exclusionary provisions:

- Regulation A: corporate offerings of less than $5 million
- Regulation D: private placements
- Rule 144: control and restricted securities
- Rule 147: securities offered and sold exclusively intrastate

Antifraud Regulations of the Acts of 1933 and 1934

Although a security might be exempt from the registration requirement and regulations regarding disclosure of information, *no offering is exempt from the antifraud provisions* of the Securities Act of 1933. The antifraud or antimanipulation provisions of the 1933 act apply to all new securities offerings, whether exempt from registration or not. Issuers must provide accurate information regarding any securities offered to the public.

Exemptions from the act of 1934. Securities exempt from registration under the act of 1933 are not subject to most of the Securities Exchange Act of 1934's rules and regulations regarding trading, proxy solicitation, insider trading or margin requirements. As with the act of 1933, however, no security is exempt from the act of 1934's antifraud and market manipulation regulations.

State Registration of New Issues

Agents and broker-dealers must be registered before they can offer or sell any security in a state. However, registration of the persons involved in the offer or the sale often is not enough to make the transaction legal. The security itself must be registered, too, unless that type of security or the transaction involved is exempt from the registration requirement.

According to the Uniform Securities Act, no person can offer or sell any security in a state lawfully unless the:

- security is registered under the Uniform Securities Act;
- security is designated by the act as exempt from the registration requirement; or
- transaction is designated by the act as exempt from the registration requirement.

If a security is not exempt from the registration requirement, the security is called a *nonexempt security*.

Types of Securities Registrations

The Uniform Securities Act provides for three types of registrations for nonexempt securities: registration by coordination, registration by filing and registration by qualification.

Registration by Coordination

Registration by coordination involves coordinating a state registration with a federal registration. Coordination is the state registration of an initial public offering. If an application to register a security with the SEC under the Securities Act of 1933 currently is pending, the security may be registered simultaneously with the state administrator of the Uniform Securities Act.

Registration by coordination is accomplished by filing a registration statement containing the following information:

- three copies of the latest prospectus;
- if the administrator requires it, copies of the articles of incorporation or bylaws, any agreements among underwriters, any indenture, a specimen of the security and any other necessary information; and
- any amendments to the prospectus that are filed with the SEC.

The registration statement must reveal the amount of the securities to be offered in the state and list the other states in which the offering will be filed. Any amendments made in the federal registration also must be made in the state registration.

If the administrator does not rule to the contrary and if the registration statement has been on file for 10 days and no stop orders are in effect, the registration becomes effective at the same time as the federal registration.

Registration by Filing

To be eligible to register securities by filing, the corporation must be an established issuer and must meet stringent financial requirements. Therefore, registration by filing is available for the registration of an issuer's additional shares. The issuer may use registration by filing to coincide with the effective date of a federal registration statement or to extend into an additional state its legal sales territory for an offering that the SEC has already cleared. The issuer notifies the administrator of its intent to offer and sell the securities in the state and supplies documents demonstrating that the issuer:

- has been in continuous operation for at least 36 consecutive calendar months;
- has previously registered an equity offering with the SEC (currently, the stock must be held by at least 500 persons, and at least 400,000 shares must be held by members of the public, not insiders);
- has a minimum total net worth of $4 million;
- has filed all material the SEC requires for at least 36 months;
- has at least four market makers for the securities (if the registration is of equity securities);
- has not defaulted on a debt payment or failed to pay a preferred dividend within the past fiscal year; and
- is offering securities at a price of at least $5 per share.

Registration by filing also requires that each participating underwriter be a member of an association of securities dealers, contract to purchase the securities as a principal and receive a commission or discount of not more than 10 percent of the securities' aggregate offering price. Registration by filing is accomplished by filing a registration statement containing the following information:

- statement as to the firm's eligibility for registration
- description of the security being offered
- issuer's name, address and form of organization
- copy of the offering circular or prospectus

Unless the administrator or the SEC issues a stop order, a registration by filing becomes effective concurrently with the effectiveness of the federal registration statement (or after five days, if the federal registration is already effective).

Registration by Qualification

Registration by qualification is the most complex means of registering an issue in a state and involves the filing of all required registration statements with a state administrator to qualify an issue of securities. Any security may be registered by this method, and all nonexempt securities not eligible for registration by some other procedure must be registered by qualification. A security that needs to be registered in only one state (an *intrastate* security) most likely will be registered by qualification.

Registration by qualification is accomplished by filing a registration statement containing the following information:

- issuer's name, address and form of organization;
- general character and nature of its business;
- description of its physical properties and equipment;
- statement of conditions of the industry or business in which it intends to engage;
- name, address and occupation of every director and officer of the issuer and every owner of 10 percent or more of the issuer's securities, the amount of the issuer's securities the person owns and the amount of remuneration paid him during the last 12 months;
- issuer's capitalization and long-term debt;
- kind and amount of securities to be offered, the proposed offering price and the aggregate selling and underwriting discounts;
- estimated cash proceeds and purpose for which the proceeds will be used;
- copies of any prospectus, pamphlet, circular, form letter, advertisement or other sales literature intended to be used with the offering;
- specimen of the security being registered;
- balance sheet from within four months of the filing; and
- any additional information the administrator requires.

The administrator has the power to require any information he decides is necessary before registering the security.

A registration by qualification becomes effective whenever the administrator so orders.

State Registration Provisions

A number of general provisions apply to all forms of state securities registration. Among these provisions are the following:

- The state administrator sets filing fees for registrations of securities. If a security is withdrawn from registration before it becomes effective, the administrator normally retains a specified amount of the fee paid.
- If the issuer has filed a registration for a similar security within the previous five years, the issuer may reference the previously filed documents in the current registration statement if the documents are still current and accurate. The administrator has the power to permit the issuer to omit any item of information from the required registration documentation.
- A securities registration is effective for one year from its effective date unless the underwriters are still attempting to distribute unsold shares, in which case the registration's effectiveness will be extended until the shares are sold.

- While the registration is effective, the administrator may require the persons who filed the registration to file reports not more often than quarterly, to keep the registration statement current and to disclose the offering's progress.

Under the provisions of the National Securities Markets Improvement Act of 1996, the states no longer exercise certain controls over securities registration. This provision was adopted under the USA. The SEC now regulates:

- securities registration of investment companies
- disclosure documents (such as prospectuses)
- proxies
- annual reports

Although states no longer exercise control over those activities or communications, they still must enforce all applicable antifraud laws and regulations. The states also continue to receive filing fees from the issuers.

Denial, Suspension or Revocation of Securities Registration

An administrator may issue a stop order denying, suspending or revoking the effectiveness of any securities registration, whether by filing, coordination or qualification, if he finds it in the public interest to do so and he finds that:

- the registration statement is misleading or incomplete
- any officer of the issuer has been convicted of a securities crime
- the security is subject to court injunction
- the offering is fraudulent
- offering expenses or promoter's fees are excessive or unreasonable

Exemptions from State Registration

Covered Securities

The Securities Act of 1933 now exempts "covered securities" from state registration. This exemption was established under the NSMIA and adopted under the USA. To avoid duplicate registration of securities that are deemed to have a national interest, covered securities must be registered with the SEC only. States are not permitted to require registration of these securities. Covered securities include the following:

- securities listed on an exchange or quoted on the Nasdaq National Market System;
- shares of registered investment companies;
- securities sold to qualified purchasers; and
- offerings and transactions exempt from federal registration.

Exempt Securities

Some securities are exempt from both the registration requirements and the advertising filing requirements of the Uniform Securities Act. However, no security is exempt from the antifraud provisions of the USA or any other federal act. Securities issued by the following issuers are considered exempt under this act. (For purposes of this section, "guaranteed" means guaranteed as to payment of principal, interest or dividends.)

- **U.S. government securities**. All securities issued or guaranteed by the government of the United States, including Series EE and Series HH savings bonds and certificates of deposit (CDs), are exempt from the registration requirements of the Uniform Securities Act.
- **Municipal securities.** Securities issued or guaranteed by any state or political subdivision of any state or any agency of a state or a subdivision are exempt.
- **Any recognized foreign government securities.** All securities issued by a recognized foreign government—that is, a government with which the United States currently maintains diplomatic relations—are exempt. In addition, all securities issued not only by the national government of Canada, but also by any of the Canadian provinces or any political subdivision (such as a town), are exempt.
- **Certain financial institutions' securities.** All securities issued by and representing an interest in or a debt of any national bank or federal savings and loan association, including CDs, are exempt. Securities issued by banks, savings institutions or trust companies organized under the laws of any state also are exempt, as are securities issued by credit unions and industrial loan associations.
- **Insurance company securities.** Any security that represents an interest in or a debt of or is guaranteed by an insurance company is exempt. Variable annuities, investment contracts and similar securities with payments dependent on the performance of a segregated fund or account invested in securities are not exempt.
- **Public utility and common carrier securities.** Any security issued or guaranteed by a railroad, a trucking company or another common carrier that is subject to the jurisdiction of the Interstate Commerce Commission (ICC), or by a public utility or a holding company subject to the jurisdiction of the Public Utility Holding Company Act of 1935, is exempt.
- **Religious and charitable organization securities.** Any security issued by a religious or charitable not-for-profit organization is exempt. Individual state statutes vary widely, but educational, benevolent, fraternal and reformatory associations are other types of organizations usually included in this category.

Certain other classes of securities are exempt from the act's registration requirements.

Securities listed on national stock exchanges. All securities listed on the NYSE, the American Stock Exchange (AMEX), the Chicago Stock Exchange or another approved regional U.S. securities exchange are exempt. This exemption is sometimes referred to as the *blue chip exemption*. Securities that are unlisted but that are admitted to unlisted trading privileges on a national exchange are also exempt.

Nasdaq-quoted securities. Certain Nasdaq-quoted (National Association of Securities Dealers Automated Quotation system-quoted) securities are now exempt in 26 states. Nasdaq is the electronic quotation system for OTC securities. To qualify for quoting on the Nasdaq system, an OTC security must meet specific standards. For example, the company issuing the security must have total assets of $2 million or more, and at least 100,000 shares of the company's stock must be publicly held. Two states do not require registration of Nasdaq securities, and one state automatically registers Nasdaq securities.

Commercial paper. Promissory notes, bankers' acceptances, drafts and other types of short-term notes with one of the top three ratings, maturities of nine months (270 days) or less and denominations of at least $50,000 are exempt.

Employee pension and profit-sharing or savings plans. Investment contracts issued in connection with employee profit-sharing, savings or similar benefit plans are exempt if the state administrator is notified in writing at least 30 days before the commencement of such a plan.

Exempt Transactions

The following transactions are exempt from the registration and advertising filing requirements of the Uniform Securities Act, but not from its antifraud provisions.

Isolated nonissuer transactions. All isolated nonissuer transactions, whether effected through a broker-dealer or not, are exempt. A nonissuer transaction is any transaction that does not directly or indirectly benefit an issuer; that is, the securities are traded between members of the public through a broker-dealer. Initial (primary) offerings are considered issuer transactions. Transactions in the secondary market are considered nonissuer transactions.

"Isolated" means one or very few transactions within the state per broker-dealer per year. The exact number varies by state. Agents should be cautioned that the philosophy that "an occasional sale is OK for me" is very dangerous. The agent must check carefully the firm's compliance authority before entering an order on the premise that it is an isolated transaction.

Nonissuer transactions in outstanding securities. Nonissuer transactions in outstanding securities (securities already publicly held) are exempt if either of the following two conditions is met:

- A recognized securities manual (such as Moody's, Standard & Poor's, Fitch's or Best's) contains certain information about the issuer. This exemption is commonly referred to as a *manual exemption*. The manual must contain the names of the issuer's officers and directors, a balance sheet of the issuer dated within the last 18 months and an income statement for the most recent calendar or fiscal year.

- The security has a fixed maturity or a fixed interest or dividend provision and has not defaulted during the preceding four years (including the current year) or for the life of the issuer, whichever is less.

For example, an individual who purchases IBM shares would be effecting a nonissuer transaction in outstanding securities.

Unsolicited orders. Unsolicited nonissuer transactions effected through a broker-dealer are exempt. State laws or a state administrator may dictate what securities transactions an agent may or may not solicit. This same limitation cannot be placed on the general public; however, a client may purchase any security she chooses.

How does an agent legally fill an order for a client who wishes to purchase a security that is nonexempt, does not appear in a recognized manual and does not qualify under isolated sales provisions? It is a good business practice to have the client acknowledge in writing the order's unsolicited status. Under the USA, the state administrator may require the client to sign an acknowledgment that the order was unsolicited. Unsolicited orders are exempt transactions, but the agent must be prepared to carry the burden of proof.

Issuer transactions. Transactions between issuers and underwriters are exempt.

Transactions by certain persons. "Fiduciary" refers to a person responsible for something held in trust for another person. Any transaction by a fiduciary is exempt from state security regulations. Fiduciary transactions include those by an executor, an administrator, a sheriff, a marshall, a receiver, a trustee in bankruptcy, a guardian or a conservator.

Pledges. A margin account transaction in which the investing customer's securities are *pledged* by the broker-dealer to a lending bank for the funds necessary to complete the trade. This process is known as *hypothecation*.

Transactions with financial institutions. This exemption is known as the *sophisticated* (or *professional*) *investor transaction exemption*. The Uniform Securities Act is designed to protect the general public, not to limit the activities of informed professional investors, institutional buyers and broker-dealers, including:

- banks
- savings institutions
- trust companies
- insurance companies
- registered investment companies
- pension or profit-sharing trusts
- broker-dealers

Transactions with these financial institutions are exempt whether the institutions act for their own accounts or for the accounts of others.

Private placements. A private placement is simply a sale of nonexempt securities that is not made to the general public. In a private placement, registration of the security is not necessary. However, the Uniform Securities Act does stipulate the following requirements for private placements:

- The number of people receiving offers, other than financial or institutional investors or broker-dealers, must be restricted to 10 in any 12-month period.
- All sales must be made to buyers who purchase for the purpose of investment.
- No commissions or fees may be paid directly or indirectly for soliciting noninstitutional buyers.

Preorganization certificates. A preorganization certificate is an agreement to purchase shares of stock in a company not yet in existence, but to be incorporated. An offer or a sale of a preorganization certificate (or subscription) is exempt if it meets *all* of the following conditions:

- No commission or other remuneration is provided for soliciting prospective subscribers.
- The number of subscribers does not exceed 10.
- No payment is made by any subscriber.

Other exempt transactions. Other transactions are exempted under the act, including:

- underwriting transactions;
- offers to existing securities holders, including holders of convertible securities, nontransferable warrants and transferable warrants exercisable within 90 days of their issuance, provided:
  - no commission is paid for soliciting the securities holders; and
  - the issuer files with the administrator a notice of the offer that the administrator does not disallow within five full business days; and
- indications of interest.

Denial and Revocation of Exemptions

The administrator may deny or revoke an exemption if he discovers that the security's or transaction's exemption is based on fraudulent, misleading or unethical business practices and if he finds that doing so would be in the public's best interest. In any event, the burden of proving eligibility for an exemption falls to the person claiming the exemption. The administrator may, without prior notice, issue a summary order denying or revoking the exempt status of a security issued by a religious or charitable organization, or denying or revoking the exempt status of any exempt transaction, such as a private placement or a transaction with a financial institution.

Unlawful Representations

It is unlawful to make misleading statements to customers concerning the status of a security's or transaction's registration or exemption, including:

- telling customers that exchange listing of a security is anticipated, without knowing the truth about such a statement;
- telling customers that a security registered with the SEC or a state securities administrator has been approved by such regulators; and
- implying to customers that regulation by any authority, including listing on a registered stock exchange, enhances a security's safety or performance.

4 Ethics and Other Federal Legislation in the Securities Industry

Key Terms	Chinese Wall Doctrine	Securities Investor Protection Act of 1970
	churning	Securities Investor Protection
	contemporaneous trader	Corporation (SIPC)
	excessive trading	shared account
	Insider Trading Act of 1988	Telephone Consumer Protection Act
	private securities transaction	of 1991 (TCPA)

Overview

The USA's antifraud provisions apply to anyone involved in a securities transaction or anyone who receives compensation for investment advice. The antifraud provisions of the Investment Advisers Act of 1940 apply to both registered investment advisers and to any person who fits the definition of an investment adviser, whether or not that person is registered.

The Uniform Securities Act lists specific fraudulent or prohibited practices, but with the notation that the list is not all-inclusive. Each person has the responsibility of determining whether his business practices are dishonest or unethical. Some acts that would be considered fraudulent are easy to identify as such, but many are not. "Fraud" is defined as the deliberate concealment, misrepresentation or omission of material information or truth to deceive or manipulate another party for unlawful or unfair gain, whether or not the act results in a sale.

This chapter describes specific acts that constitute unethical business practices in the securities industry, as well as additional legislation that affects participants in the U.S. securities markets.

Ethical Behavior of Investment Advisers

Because of the nature of their business and the amount of trust a client must put into an advisory relationship, the standard of business ethics to which investment advisers are expected to conform is very high. As is the case with any investment or securities professional, investment advisers are prohibited from:

- employing any device, scheme or artifice to defraud;
- engaging in any fraudulent or deceitful practice or course of business;
- failing to disclose in writing the capacity in which the investment adviser acts (agent or principal) in a transaction for a client and failing to obtain the client's written consent before the transaction's completion;
- making any untrue statement of material fact or omitting a material fact; or
- engaging in any other practices the administrator defines by rule as dishonest or unethical.

Disclosure of Capacity

If the investment adviser acts as a principal in a transaction—that is, she buys securities from or sells securities to a client from her own account—she must make a written disclosure to the client of her capacity and obtain the client's consent before any such transaction. The same disclosure and consent are required if the investment adviser acts as a broker, arranging the transaction on behalf of a client.

A broker-dealer acting as an investment adviser is exempt from the disclosure of capacity requirement if it is engaged in (1) offering impersonal advisory services or (2) distributing written materials to 35 or more persons who are paying for those materials, *always provided* that the broker-dealer includes a statement in any communication to clients that, depending on the transaction and the circumstances, it *may* act as either a principal for its own account or an agent for another person.

Disclosure of Legal Action

Any material legal or disciplinary action must be disclosed to clients and prospective clients not less than 48 hours prior to entering into an investment advisory contract.

The Uniform Securities Act considers a legal or disciplinary action to be material if the finding was handed down within the past 10 years and:

- resulted in the adviser being restricted from conducting an investment-related business;
- took place in a criminal or civil court of law or was the result of a hearing with a state securities administrator, the SEC or a self-regulatory organization; and
- involved the investment adviser or a person associated with the firm who has the power to exercise influence over the firm's policies or the investment advice given.

Suitability and Investment Recommendations

Investment recommendations must be in keeping with customer needs, financial capability and objectives. Customers should be guided to investments that make sense for them, not for the registered person. The investment adviser should explain each investment fully, including its risks. At no time should customers own an investment which could put them at risk beyond their financial capacity.

Dishonest or Unethical Business Practices

Investment advisers are prohibited from engaging in any business practice or behavior that is dishonest, unethical or fraudulent. "Fraud" is commonly understood to mean making a statement while knowing it to be false and having the intention to deceive.

The state administrator in each state is authorized by the Uniform Securities Act to define unethical and dishonest behavior in whatever way is necessary to protect the interests of the investors in that state. The Uniform Securities Act also codifies NASAA's *Statement of Policy on Unethical Business Practices of Investment Advisers* and sets forth specific business practices that constitute fraudulent or deceitful methods for taking unfair advantage of customers.

Suitability. An investment adviser may not recommend a transaction to a customer without having a basis for believing the transaction to be suitable. An adviser must consider each customer's individual financial situation and investment objectives whenever he recommends a transaction. Failure to make reasonable inquiry about the customer's needs and objectives is unethical and prohibited.

Discretionary authority. Discretion is the authority to decide the security, the number of shares or units and whether to buy or sell, but not the timing or price of a transaction only. An investment adviser must not carry out discretionary transactions for or on behalf of a customer without first obtaining the customer's written authority.

Third-party authority. An investment adviser may not accept orders on behalf of a customer from individuals other than the customer without first obtaining third-person trading authority. The adviser may accept only those orders placed by the account owner or by another party who has been granted trading authorization in writing.

Excessive trading. An investment adviser must not induce trading in a client's account that is excessive in terms of size or frequency. This is a prohibited practice known as *churning*. Inducing transactions solely to generate commissions without regard to the customer's best interest or investment objectives is a form of churning.

Borrowing. An investment adviser is prohibited from borrowing money or securities from a customer, even if the customer agrees or signs a written contract, except in a few circumstances. An adviser may borrow from a customer that is an affiliate, a broker-dealer, or a bank or some other institution in the business of lending money.

Commingling. An investment adviser may not commingle (mix) a customer's funds with the adviser's own funds. The Uniform Securities Act does not prohibit an adviser or investment adviser rep from having a personal joint account with a customer or another person.

Material facts. An investment adviser may not misrepresent or omit a material fact regarding an investment or regarding the adviser's qualifications or fees. For example, an adviser may not state that the state administrator has approved his business. With regard to a particular transaction, the adviser must accurately state the amount of commission or markup or markdown to be charged. An investment adviser is also responsible for informing the customer if a certain transaction involves larger than ordinary commissions or costs.

Sources. If someone other than the investment adviser prepares a report or recommendation, the adviser or rep must disclose that fact.

Fees. An investment adviser cannot charge unreasonable fees for advisory services—that is, fees out of line in relation to fees charged by other advisers offering similar services.

Conflicts of interest. An investment adviser must disclose any material conflict of interest that could impair his objectivity. For example, an adviser must disclose an arrangement whereby the adviser receives compensation from an outside source in addition to compensation from the client receiving advisory services. Also, an adviser must disclose if he receives both a fee for investment advice and a commission for executing securities transactions based on that advice.

Customer protection. An investment adviser must comply with safekeeping requirements that protect customer funds and securities. These requirements are set forth in the Uniform Securities Act's custody rule.

Contracts. Each investment advisory contract must be in writing, disclose terms and fees, specify whether discretionary power is granted and prohibit the contract from being assigned—that is, sold or transferred to another firm—without the customer's permission.

Market Manipulation

Another type of violation is an action intended to influence the price of securities in the market. Securities industry personnel are responsible for upholding the integrity of the markets and must not engage in activities that illegally manipulate market values.

Other Unethical Practices

Regardless of whether a particular course of action of a broker-dealer, an investment adviser or a representative is specifically prohibited, these persons are always held to high ethical standards. Other business practices not specified in the Uniform Securities Act but generally agreed to be dishonest or unethical include:

- deliberately failing to follow a customer's instructions;
- effecting transactions with a customer who is not recorded on the books of the rep's employer, unless the transactions are approved in writing in advance;
- failing to bring a customer's written complaint to the attention of the rep's employer;
- soliciting orders for unregistered nonexempt securities;
- sharing in the profits or losses of a customer's account, unless the customer and the employer have given written consent and the percentage of profit or loss is the same as the percentage of the registered person's personal funds invested in the account;
- misrepresenting to customers the status of their accounts;
- promising to perform certain services for customers without intending to perform those services or being qualified to do so; and
- disseminating inaccurate or phony market quotations—any quotation that an adviser, a broker-dealer or a rep provides to a customer must be bona fide.

Other Federal Legislation

Securities Investor Protection Act of 1970

The Securities Investor Protection Corporation (SIPC) was established in 1970 with the passage of the Securities Investor Protection Act. The purpose of the act is to protect the customers of securities firms that go bankrupt. SIPC is a nonprofit corporation, not a government-sponsored corporation such as the Federal Deposit Insurance Corporation (FDIC).

Members include all broker-dealers registered under the Securities Exchange Act of 1934, all members of national securities exchanges and most NASD members.

Each separate customer at a broker-dealer firm is covered for a maximum of $500,000 in securities and cash. Of that amount, up to $100,000 in cash is covered. Equity in margin accounts is covered up to $500,000. Commodities accounts are not covered. Customers with claims beyond $500,000 are treated as general creditors on the excess amount.

A person who has several accounts in her own name at one broker-dealer firm still has maximum coverage of $500,000 because the protection is $500,000 *per separate customer, not per account*. That customer could, however, have several accounts at one broker-dealer firm in different forms of ownership.

When a member firm is in financial trouble, SIPC requests that a federal district court appoint a trustee, whose responsibilities include:

- supervising the SIPC member's orderly liquidation
- notifying clients of the liquidation
- returning clients' identifiable securities

When notified, clients file claims with the trustee to receive any monies or securities due them.

Insider Trading and Securities Fraud Enforcement Act of 1988

Policies and procedures. The Insider Trading and Securities Fraud Enforcement Act of 1988 expanded the definition of, and the liabilities and penalties for, the illicit use of nonpublic information established by the Securities Exchange Act of 1934. Insiders, including officers, directors and 10 percent shareholders, may be held liable for more than just transactions in their own accounts. The act recognizes the insider's fiduciary responsibility to the issuer, to the stockholders and to others who might be affected by trades made with insider knowledge. Investors who have suffered monetary damage because of insider trading have legal recourse against the insider and against any other party who had control over the misuse of nonpublic information.

An insider is any person who has access to nonpublic information about a corporation. Insiders may not use inside information as a basis for personal trading until that information has been made public. The SEC can levy a civil penalty of up to three times the amount of profit made or loss avoided if inside information is used. Any individual who is a corporate insider and owns securities in that corporation must file a statement of ownership with the SEC. Inside information is any information that has not been disseminated to, or is not readily available to, the general public. To determine whether information is nonpublic, the SEC considers the method by which the information is released to the public and the timing of trades relative to when other people also have the information.

Chinese Wall Doctrine

The Chinese Wall Doctrine is a descriptive name for the restrictions against sharing potentially material information between departments of a firm. Those departments or branches of a broker-dealer that have access to material nonpublic information, such as the legal department, the investment banking division and the various security analysts, may not disseminate this information to anyone who could conceivably trade on it. Firms must erect a "wall" between those who have information and those who do not in order to prevent possible violations of the law.

Written supervisory procedures. All broker-dealers must establish written supervisory procedures specifically prohibiting the use of material nonpublic information by all persons interested in, affiliated with or in any way engaged in the broker-dealers' securities-related activities. Once these procedures are established, broker-dealers must actively maintain and enforce them.

SEC investigations. The SEC has the right to investigate any person who has violated or is suspected of violating any of the provisions of the Insider Trading Act. The Commission also has the right to require anyone who has violated the act or is suspected of a violation to file a written statement with the SEC covering all of the facts and circumstances relating to the suspected violation.

The Commission also has the right to exempt anyone involved in a violation of the act from prosecution if it decides that it would be in the public interest to do so or that it would be necessary for the protection of investors.

Insider Trading Rules

The key elements of tipper and tippee liability under the insider trading rules are as follows:

- Does the tipper owe a fiduciary duty to a company or its stockholders, and has he breached it?
- Does the tipper meet the personal benefits test, even something as simple as enhancing a friendship or reputation?
- Does the tippee know or should the tippee have known that the information was inside or confidential?
- Is the information material and nonpublic?

Given these elements, a "slip of the tongue" by a corporate insider could leave that person liable under the rules, and anyone who trades on information that she knows or should know is not public is also liable.

Civil Penalties

Profits gained and losses avoided. When determining how much profit was made (or loss avoided) by the inside trader, the Commission looks at the security's market price a reasonable period after the information becomes general public knowledge. The difference between this price and the price the trader obtained is the profit or loss against which penalties are set.

Control. It is important to establish who had control over the violation or the person who committed the violation. A controlling person who knew of the violation is just as liable as the person who actually committed the misuse of nonpublic information.

Limitations to this liability exist. The simple fact that a person normally has control over another, such as the control a branch manager has over a registered rep, does not imply guilt. The Commission establishes the full extent of a person's control and involvement before it exacts any penalties.

Disgorging short-swing profits. Insiders may not retain short-swing profits (those occurring in six months or less) in securities; any short-swing profit must be repaid (disgorged) by the insider. Insiders are prohibited from establishing short-against-the-box positions and entering short sales. Any trading of insider-owned securities must be reported to the SEC within 10 days of the trade.

Criminal Penalties

The criminal penalties for violations of securities laws were increased through an amendment to the act of 1934. If a person is convicted of willfully violating federal securities regulations or of knowingly making false or misleading statements in any registration document, that person can be fined up to $1 million, sentenced to prison for up to 10 years or both. The maximum fine is $2.5 million for other than a natural person.

Contemporaneous Traders

Any person who has entered trades that have violated the insider trading regulations or who has communicated material nonpublic information to someone who has violated these regulations may be liable to contemporaneous traders and may be sued in a court of law. The concept of **contemporaneous traders** is a relatively recent addition to federal securities regulation. A contemporaneous trader is any person who enters a trade at or near the same time and in the same security as a person who has inside information.

Statute of limitations. A lawsuit can be brought in court by anyone who, at the same time, bought (if the insider sold) or sold (if the insider bought) securities of the same class. The suit may be initiated up to five years after the violation, and the damages imposed under a lawsuit of this kind can go up to the profits the insider made or the losses he avoided.

Procedures for collection. If the Commission imposes a monetary penalty for violations of the 1988 act, the penalty is payable directly to the Treasury of the United States. The U.S. attorney general has been given the authority and responsibility to collect any penalties imposed and may do so through the U.S. district courts if necessary.

Misuse of Nonpublic Information

The Investment Advisers Act of 1940 established strict regulations concerning the use and misuse of nonpublic information. Every investment adviser must establish, maintain and enforce written policies and procedures devoted to preventing violations of the rules covering nonpublic (inside) information.

Telephone Communications with the Public

The Telephone Consumer Protection Act of 1991 (TCPA), administered by the Federal Communications Commission (FCC), was enacted to protect consumers from unwanted telephone solicitations. A telephone solicitation is defined as a telephone call initiated for the purpose of encouraging the purchase of or investment in property, goods or services. The act governs commercial calls, recorded solicitations from autodialers, and solicitations and advertisements to facsimile machines and modems (E-mail). The act requires any organization that performs telemarketing (in particular, cold calling)—including a broker-dealer—to:

- maintain a "do-not-call list" of customers who do not want to be called and keep a customer's name on the list for 10 years from the time the request is made;
- institute a written policy (available on demand) on maintenance procedures for the "do-not-call list";
- train reps on using the list;
- ensure that reps acknowledge and immediately record the names and telephone numbers of customers who ask not to be called again;
- ensure that anyone making cold calls for the firm informs the customer of the firm's name and telephone number or address;
- ensure that telemarketers do not call customers within 10 years of a do-not-call request; and
- ensure that telephone solicitations occur between the hours of 8:00 am and 9:00 pm of the time zone in which a customer is located.

The act exempts calls made:

- to parties with whom the caller has an established business relationship or where the caller has prior express permission or invitation;
- on behalf of a tax-exempt nonprofit organization;
- for no commercial purpose; and
- for legitimate debt collection purposes.

Uniform Securities Act Review Exam

In questions 1 through 21, write "T" (true) if the phrase fits the definition of a security and write "F" (false) if it does not.

1. _____ U.S. Treasury bond

2. _____ Annuity that pays the same amount of money each month

3. _____ Annuity that pays a varying amount of money each month

4. _____ Certificate of interest in a profit-sharing agreement

5. _____ Keogh (HR-10) plan

6. _____ Collateral trust certificate

7. _____ Preorganization certificate

8. _____ Savings and loan account passbook

9. _____ Interest in an oil and gas drilling program

10. _____ Interest in a real estate condominium

11. _____ Term insurance policy

12. _____ Interest in farmland or animals

13. _____ Final prospectus for an oil and gas corporation

14. _____ Option contract for wheat

15. _____ Interest in a whiskey warehouse receipt

16. _____ Evidence of indebtedness, such as an interest in a condominium pool

17. _____ American Express money order

18. _____ Written confirmation of a sale of AT&T common stock

19. _____ Interest in a multilevel distributorship arrangement

20. _____ Interest in a merchandise marketing plan

21. _____ Interest in an oil, gas or mining title or lease, or in payments out of production under such a title or lease

In questions 22 through 27, write "T" (true) if the phrase fits the definition of a person and write "F" (false) if it does not.

22. _____ Unincorporated investment club

23. _____ Canadian national government

24. _____ State of New York

25. _____ Microscam, Inc.

26. _____ Individual investor

27. _____ Securities brokerage firm

In questions 28 through 31, write "T" (true) if the phrase fits the definition of a nonissuer transaction and write "F" (false) if it does not.

28. _____ Primary transaction

29. _____ Transaction between persons on a stock exchange

30. _____ Stock offering by Kelptek, Inc.

31. _____ Trade between two OTC brokers

In questions 32 through 36, write "T" (true) if the person described must register as a broker-dealer and write "F" (false) if not.

32. _____ Person who has no place of business in the state and deals exclusively with 10 institutional clients

33. _____ Person who has no place of business in the state and deals exclusively with other broker-dealers

34. _____ Person who has no place of business in the state and effects transactions exclusively with issuers of securities

35. _____ Person who has no place of business in the state and directs an offer to an existing customer with less than 30 days' temporary residency.

36. _____ Brokerage firm doing retail business in the state

In questions 37 through 44 concerning agents as defined by the Uniform Securities Act, write "T" if the statement is true and write "F" if the statement is false.

37. _____ An agent is a broker-dealer.

38. _____ The term "agent" includes an individual who effects transactions in municipal securities for a broker-dealer.

39. _____ The term "agent" includes an individual who represents an issuer in effecting transactions in six-month commercial paper.

40. _____ An agent can only be an individual.

41. _____ The term "agent" includes an individual who effects transactions in common stocks.

42. _____ An agent who represents an issuer in effecting transactions with savings institutions or trust companies is not an agent and does not have to register.

43. _____ A partner of a broker-dealer is an agent if she attempts to effect securities transactions, but is not successful at the attempts.

44. _____ The term "agent" includes a person who represents an issuer in a transaction with an underwriter.

In questions 45 through 49, write "T" (true) if the security could be sold to the public legally by an individual who represents the issuer but who is not a registered agent and write "F" (false) if the security could not be sold to the public legally by such an individual.

45. _____ Common stock issued by Mountain Brewing of Canada

46. _____ Bonds issued by the Canadian government

47. _____ Debentures issued by Worthmore, Moola Savings and Loan

48. _____ Commercial paper with a six-month maturity

49. _____ Preferred stock listed on stock exchanges

In questions 50 through 56, write "T" (true) if the phrase fits the definition of an investment adviser as defined under the USA and write "F" (false) if it does not.

50. _____ Bank that specifically sells portfolio and investment advice

51. _____ Accountant who designs a portfolio approach for a client to include tax strategies, and charges for this service

52. _____ Broker-dealer that helps a client construct a suitable portfolio and charges a small fee for this service

53. _____ Person who sells to subscribers his own investment advice letter on specific investments and who has no direct contact with the subscribers

54. _____ Publisher of a business news magazine with national circulation

55. _____ Person who sells investment advice regarding U.S. government securities

56. _____ Person acting as an investment adviser who has not been designated by the state administrator as exempt

In questions 57 through 59 concerning issuers, write "T" if the statement is true and write "F" if it is false.

57. _____ In a new offering of shares of Acme Sweatsocks, Inc., the company itself would be considered the issuer.

58. _____ The term "issuer" does not distinguish between persons who issue and persons who propose to issue securities.

59. _____ When Kelptek, Inc. issues bonds, the president of the corporation is considered an issuer.

60. What is a transaction called when there is no benefit to the issuer?

A. Primary transaction
B. Nonprofit transaction
C. Issuer transaction
D. Nonissuer transaction

61. What is the official designation of the person or agency that enforces the Uniform Securities Act in each state?

A. Transfer agent
B. Registrar
C. Issuer
D. Administrator

62. What does "guaranteed" mean when the word is used to describe a security?

A. The broker-dealer will buy the security back at the same price or higher.
B. The security has been cleared and is backed by the SEC.
C. The security has a backer that guarantees the payment of principal and interest.
D. The security is an annuity product that guarantees a retirement income.

63. What is the difference between an offer and a sale?

   A. An offer is the attempt to sell, and a sale is a binding contract to transfer a security for value.
   B. An offer is a binding proposal to sell, and a sale is a nonbinding proposal to sell.
   C. An offer can be made only by a customer, and a sale can be made only by a broker-dealer.
   D. An offer must be approved by a branch manager, and a sale needs no approval.

64. What is the smallest order that can be placed for an institutional account?

   A. $50,000 or 1,000 shares
   B. $100,000 or 2,500 shares
   C. $100,000 or 5,000 shares
   D. There is no limit on institutional order sizes.

In questions 65 through 67 concerning the registration of broker-dealers, write "T" if the statement is true and write "F" if it is false.

65. _____ The administrator may require minimum net capital for broker-dealers.

66. _____ The administrator may require a surety bond.

67. _____ Officers of a broker-dealer may be required to take registration examinations after the broker-dealer is registered in a state.

In questions 68 through 72 concerning the registration of agents, write "T" if the statement is true and write "F" if it is false.

68. _____ When an agent changes his place of employment, only the new employer is responsible for notifying the administrator.

69. _____ The Uniform Securities Agent State Law Examination is accepted by most states, which means that the administrators will have no further examination requirements for agents.

70. _____ An agent's license is effective only while the agent represents a registered broker-dealer.

71. _____ The registration of a broker-dealer automatically registers every partner, officer and director of the same firm as an agent.

72. _____ An agent representing a broker-dealer lives in one state and would like to do business in another state. No registration is necessary in the other state as long as the agent's activities are limited exclusively to effecting transactions in certain securities exempted under the Uniform Securities Act.

73. Under the national de minimis, investment advisers are exempt from state registration if they solicit how many clients within the year?

   A. Less than 6
   B. Less than 10
   C. Less than 25
   D. Less than 30

In questions 74 through 75, write "T" (true) if the person may transact business legally as an investment adviser in that state and write "F" (false) if he may not.

74. _____ The person is not registered, and his clientele is limited to banks and individuals.

75. _____ The person is registered as a broker-dealer only, and gives investment advice for special compensation beyond the scope of her broker-dealer practice.

In questions 76 through 79 concerning registration procedures, write "T" if the statement is true and write "F" if it is false.

76. _____ An application is the only document that needs to be filed if a broker-dealer, an agent or an investment adviser is to be granted registration by the state administrator.

77. _____ An application must contain whatever information the administrator requires.

78. _____ An applicant's financial condition and history are not registration considerations.

79. _____ An applicant's proposed method of doing business is a registration consideration.

In questions 80 and 81 concerning post-licensing requirements, write "T" if the statement is true and write "F" if it is false.

80. _____ Unless the administrator rules otherwise, the investment adviser of a registered investment company must maintain records for three years.

81. _____ Sales materials and advertisements for registered investment companies must be filed with the administrator before they are used.

82. The National Securities Markets Improvement Act of 1996 affected federal and state laws in which of the following ways?

A. The Uniform Securities Act will now supersede the Investment Advisers Act of 1940.
B. Federal law will preempt state law.
C. State law will preempt federal law.
D. Federal law and state law will remain the same.

83. Which of the following is a type of security registration that allows the administrator to require any information he decides is necessary?

A. Coordination
B. Filing
C. Qualification
D. Modulation

84. Which of the following is a type of state security registration that is used when a security is being registered simultaneously with the SEC under the Securities Act of 1933?

A. Coordination
B. Qualification
C. Implementation
D. Integration

85. Which of the following require(s) no specific response from the state administrator before the securities registration becomes effective?

I. Coordination
II. Filing
III. Qualification
IV. Conjugation

A. I
B. I and II
C. II, III and IV
D. II and IV

In questions 86 through 100, write "E" if the security is exempt and write "NE" if the security is nonexempt.

86. _____ Over-the-counter call option

87. _____ Security issued by the national government of Germany

88. _____ Security issued by a province of Canada

89. _____ Security issued by a political subdivision of Mexico

90. _____ U.S. Treasury note

91. _____ Church bond

92. _____ Commercial paper

93. _____ U.S. Treasury bill

94. _____ First offering of stock issued by a manufacturing company

95. _____ Stock issued by Madre Merryl Federal Savings and Loan Association

96. _____ Common stock in Seven Seas Freightways

97. _____ Stock listed exclusively on the London Stock Exchange

98. _____ Preferred stock issued by Amalgamated Featherbedders of Canada and listed on the NYSE

99. _____ Certain Nasdaq securities in certain states

100. _____ Interest in warehouse receipts

In questions 101 through 111 concerning exempt transactions under the Uniform Securities Act, write "T" if the statement is true and write "F" if it is false.

101. _____ An agent is not required to be registered in a state if the transaction he solicits is exempt.

102. _____ A private placement is a method of selling nonregistered securities.

103. _____ A sale to a sophisticated investor, such as an insurance company, is an exempt transaction whether or not the security sold is exempt.

104. _____ An agent may solicit orders in unregistered securities if his clients will sign statements that orders are unsolicited.

105. _____ An agent may execute secondary trades in nonexempt unregistered securities if he limits the number of transactions to no more than 10 in any 12-month period.

106. _____ A manual exemption allows a security to be offered even if it is not registered in a state.

107. _____ A manual exemption provides for an exempt transaction. It does not make the security itself exempt.

108. _____ Unsolicited orders are exempt transactions.

109. _____ All executor transactions are exempt.

110. _____ No commissions may be charged in a private placement if the transaction is to qualify as an exempt transaction.

111. _____ A private placement involves the sale of exempt securities.

In questions 112 through 125, indicate whether you think the action described is lawful or unlawful and explain your decision.

112. ALFA Enterprises paid four quarterly dividends of $.25 each during the last calendar year. In addition, it paid a special $1 year-end dividend because of an extraordinary item of income. An agent informs his client that owning ALF shares should provide an ever-increasing income in the form of dividends because of the dramatic increase authorized by the board at year-end.

_____

_____

Use the following information to answer questions 113 through 116. Three years ago, General Gizmonics, Inc. earned $2 per share. Two years ago, earnings dropped to $1 per share. Last year, the earnings per share were $2. Analysts have projected earnings of $3 per share this year.

	EPS	% Change
Estimate for this year	$3	50%
Actual, last year	$2	100%
Actual, two years ago	$1	– 50%
Actual, three years ago	$2	0%

113. An agent tells his client that earnings have increased at an average rate of 75 percent.

_____

_____

114. An agent tells his client that earnings dropped 50 percent two years ago, increased 100 percent last year and are expected to rise another 50 percent this year. Earnings, he states, thus show an average increase of 33 1/3 percent a year.

_____

_____

115. An agent tells his client that earnings were $2 per share three years ago and are expected to reach $3 per share this year. He says a 50 percent increase over a four-year period averages to 12.5 percent per year.

_____

_____

116. An agent tells his client that he likes the potential of General Gizmonics over the long term, but points out that there is quite a bit of risk associated with buying the stock. He explains the risk of using simple averages when discussing the company's earnings and illustrates his point by showing the client that there was a 50 percent reduction in earnings two years ago and that the 100 percent increase in earnings last year offset the earlier reduction.

_____

_____

117. An agent tells his client that the net earnings figure is the best indicator of a particular company's progress because recent stock offerings distort comparisons on a per-share basis.

_____

_____

118. An agent tells his client that a company has finally "graduated" to the level of quality acceptable to the New York Stock Exchange. He recommends the stock to the client based on the Exchange's stringent earnings requirements for listing.

_____

_____

119. An agent informs his client that he thinks the common stock of a company will be listed on a national securities exchange. The agent is basing his prediction on his "feel" for the market.

_____

_____

120. An agent offers a stock to a client with no markup or commission. The current quote is 14–14 1/2. The client's order is filled at 14 3/4.

_____

_____

121. An agent informs his client that SEC and state approval finally have been received on a new issue so that an offering now can be released.

_____

_____

122. The credit department of a broker-dealer calls one of the agents to inform him that margin requirements dictate that one of his clients deposit $2,000. Knowing that the client does not have $2,000 excess cash at this time, the agent calls the client and suggests that the client sell shares of one of his securities in the margin account. The agent thinks this sale would meet the margin call and at the same time make it unnecessary to worry the customer by informing him of the margin call.

_____

_____

123. As a standard part of his prospecting presentation, an agent promises each of his prospects that he will supply him with copies of each item he sees in all of the major financial publications that have to do with the client's security positions. Normally, the agent does not have time for this, but every few months, when business is slow, he sends out a few items.

_____

_____

124. As a standard part of his prospecting presentation, an agent promises to perform all tax services and portfolio analysis for a client. He took a tax course in college, but knows he is not always up on current laws and generally tries to avoid filling out clients' forms unless they really push for it.

_____

_____

125. An agent offers a security to his client, and the offer is accepted. The trade is executed at $27 per share. One week later, the stock is trading at $20 per share and the agent does not want to inform his client of this fact. He tells the client that the price of the stock is still in the $27 area, but circumstances have changed and the client should liquidate now to avoid a loss. When the liquidation is executed at $20, the agent calls the client and apologizes for the precipitous drop in price just prior to the client's taking advantage of the agent's astute advice.

     _____

     _____

In questions 126 and 127 concerning what constitutes the fraudulent or misleading omission of material facts, indicate whether you think the action described is lawful or unlawful and explain your decision.

126. An agent wants to make a short but efficient presentation to a number of clients, but realizes that he cannot cover everything. To save time, he deliberately "sorts out" material facts regarding a company he is recommending.

     _____

     _____

127. At a time of a 50 percent margin, a client buys $20,000 worth of securities with a deposit of $10,000 cash. When he makes the purchase, the client informs the agent that he cannot afford a loss that would exceed $4,000. Later, trading is halted in the stock owing to an influx of sale orders. When the stock reopens, the market value has dropped in half and a margin call is sent to the client in the amount of $3,000. When informed that he is down $10,000 on paper, the client is stunned. He cannot understand how he has lost all of his money and still needs to pay an additional $3,000.

     _____

     _____

In questions 128 and 129 concerning the fraudulent or deceitful use of material inside information, indicate whether you think the action described is lawful or unlawful and explain your decision.

128. While visiting a publicly held corporation, an agent overhears that the company has just lost its largest client to a competitor. Because of this knowledge, the agent decides to discontinue his efforts to sell the common stock of this corporation.

     _____

     _____

129. An agent hears from a friend that a publicly held company has just lost its largest client to a competitor. He decides to sell the stock short in his brother's account.

     _____

     _____

In questions 130 through 134 concerning the requirement that agents' recommendations and transactions be suitable for individual clients, indicate whether you think the action described is lawful or unlawful and explain your decision.

130. An 80-year-old man with limited resources wants to purchase shares of a speculative new company. Before his agent asks any questions, the man informs him that he will buy the stock either from him or from another agent across the street. The agent opens a new account and enters the order marked "unsolicited."

_____

_____

131. An agent with a large clientele of individual investors decides to recommend that each client purchase shares of stock in a new company that has expertise in the area of solar power.

_____

_____

132. An agent sells 1,000 shares of a $50 security to a new account. One week later, he finds that the customer does not have enough funds to make the full payment.

_____

_____

133. One agent has been following the recommendations of another agent in the office because each of the other agent's recommendations has had an impressive performance. Therefore, as soon as the second agent begins selling a new investment idea, the first agent picks up the phone and offers it to all of his clients, too.

_____

_____

134. In the last week of the commission month, an agent recommends the sale of FLB and purchase of DOH to clients who own FLB. To clients who own DOH, he recommends the sale of DOH and the purchase of FLB.

_____

_____

In questions 135 through 137, use the following information and indicate whether you think the action described is lawful or unlawful; explain your decision.

An agent hears from another agent a rumor about a possible buyout of Greater Health, Inc. at book value. The book value of the company is $15 per share and the current market value is $10 per share.

135. The agent calls several clients and suggests purchase because of an impending buyout at $15 per share.

_____

_____

136. The agent discusses the rumor with his branch manager to determine what action, if any, could be taken.

_____

_____

137. The agent takes a careful look at Greater Health, Inc. He decides the investment merit of GHI is good regardless of a buyout and begins recommending it to some of his clients. He does not include any reference to the potential buyout and feels that, if it does happen, it would be a pleasant surprise for the clients who own the stock.

_____

_____

In questions 138 through 149 concerning prohibited business practices, indicate whether you think the action described is lawful or unlawful and explain your decision.

138. An agent opens an individual account for Randy Bear. By way of a referral from Randy, the agent also opens an individual account for Hugh Heifer, who is Randy's partner. Both Randy and Hugh purchase identical portfolios from the agent. In a telephone conversation, Randy informs the agent that one particular security should be liquidated from each individual account. The agent does this.

_____

_____

139. An agent receives an unsolicited order from a client to purchase shares of an obscure foreign merchant bank. After days of toil and transatlantic telephone calls, the exhausted trader triumphantly reports an execution. In addition to the usual commission charge, the broker-dealer adds the cost of the telephone calls. The client balks, feeling that the charges should be absorbed by the broker-dealer as a cost of doing business.

_____

_____

140. Ada Bullwether, a lifelong friend and neighbor of an agent, also happens to be that agent's largest client. During one particularly bad downturn in the market, the agent is faced with a margin call he cannot meet without liquidating some of the securities in his account. Mrs. Bullwether offers to transfer cash and securities from her own account into the agent's account. Rather than accept this offer, the agent has a legal and binding loan agreement drawn up and borrows $10,000 from Mrs. Bullwether.

_____

_____

141. An agent has a good client who is on vacation in Europe. While the client is gone, two limit orders fill, resulting in a net amount due from the client of $750. The agent knows the client is not a poor credit risk, but is unable to contact him. The agent deposits his own check for $750 so that the client is not sold out because of Federal Reserve Board regulations. Later, when the client returns from Europe, he gives the agent his check for $750.

_____

_____

142. A customer calls his agent and informs him that he must liquidate a security today. The customer has to have the funds available to him a week later, when an important business transaction is to be completed. The agent, rather than entering the sell order immediately, holds the order off until later in the day to get his customer a better price. As luck would have it, trading activity is suspended in the stock during the afternoon because of an impending news announcement. Several days later, it is learned that the stock probably will never open again because of bankruptcy proceedings.

_____

_____

143. An agent frantically tries to reach his customer regarding bad news about one of the customer's security positions. Finally, even though he cannot contact the customer, the agent enters an order to liquidate the security because he knows it is in the customer's best interest.

_____

_____

144. An agent enters an order from a person who, until now, has not been a client. He writes "new account" on the order form and turns in the new account information at the end of the trading day.

_____

_____

145. A client writes a blistering letter to an agent regarding stocks that the agent had recommended and that subsequently have performed very poorly. The agent decides not to forward the letter to his supervisor because he knows the analyst involved already is aware that he misread the market.

_____

_____

146. A client informs his agent that he wants to buy one share of each of the 30 companies that make up the Dow Jones Industrial Average. The client is shocked when he discovers that the agent's employer has charged $25 commission per share. He does not feel any better when he finds out that it is the employing broker-dealer's policy to charge a minimum of $25 commission on each order.

_____

_____

147. An agent sells his client 10 U.S. government bonds due to mature in 30 years. The agent tells the client that he has chosen these securities because there is "no way you can lose money on the safest security on earth."

_____

_____

148. An agent with extensive personal resources knows that a particular technical analyst is waiting for 20,000 shares of Quantum Rapid Search, Inc. stock to trade in one day before he recommends the security. Just for the fun of it, the agent buys 10,000 shares in the morning and sells 10,000 shares in the afternoon of the same day. Seeing the volume of the stock finally hitting 20,000 shares, the technical analyst promptly issues his buy recommendation.

_____

_____

149. An agent actively solicits orders for a new underwriting in his home state. The next day, he learns that the underwriting is not registered in his home state. Now, feeling lucky that his sales efforts have gone unrewarded, he ceases soliciting orders in this nonexempt security.

_____

_____

In questions 150 through 155, write "Y" (yes) if the action is in compliance with the Uniform Securities Act and write "N" (no) if it is not.

150. _____ An investment adviser assigns an advisory contract after providing written notice to the client.

151. _____ An adviser notifies his client that the president of the advisory corporation has left to start his own business.

152. _____ An investment adviser and his client enter into a contract that calls for the adviser to receive a fee of $10,000 plus 30 percent of any profits or less 40 percent of any losses.

153. _____ An investment adviser and his client enter into a contract that calls for the adviser to receive a fee of $10,000 or 1/2 percent of the average annual assets, whichever is greater.

154. _____ An investment adviser takes custody of a client's securities and money with no further action on the adviser's part. There is no rule against such activity and he has a written contract with the client.

155. _____ A new investment adviser that as of yet has no customers notifies the administrator that it intends to have custody of customer assets. There is no rule against such activity.

156. Which of the following would justify an administrator's denial of a security's registration?

   I. The order is in the public interest.
   II. The company has not been paying dividends.
   III. The underwriter's compensation is excessive.

   A. I
   B. I and II
   C. I and III
   D. III

157. Which of the following would justify an administrator's suspension of an agent's registration?

   I. The order is in the public interest.
   II. The agent has been found guilty of a felony.
   III. The agent is being sued by a client.

   A. I only
   B. I and II only
   C. II only
   D. I, II and III

In questions 158 through 162, write "T" if the statement is true and write "F" if it is false.

158. _____ The administrator must give notice of his orders to persons negatively affected.

159. _____ Any person negatively affected by an order of an administrator must be offered a hearing.

160. _____ Suspension of an agent is reason enough for an administrator to suspend automatically the agent's entire firm.

161. _____ Suspension of an officer or a director of a brokerage firm does not authorize the administrator to proceed against the entire firm.

162. _____ If the administrator finds that it is in the public interest to do so, he may deny an investment adviser's registration on the grounds of lack of experience.

163. Which of the following would exonerate the seller from civil suit resulting from an illegal sale made in a state?

A. The seller offers to buy back the security sold.
B. The security sold pays income that exceeds 6 percent.
C. The buyer already has disposed of the security.
D. The seller reimburses the buyer for any losses incurred within one year.

164. An agent works for a brokerage firm in Illinois, and his client lives in Illinois. The agent makes an offer to the client by phone while the client is vacationing in California. The client accepts the offer while still in California. The client travels to Texas before returning home and sends payment for the security from there. He makes his payment by sending a check from a money-market fund based in Ohio. The administrator(s) of which state(s) have authority over the sale?

I. Illinois
II. California
III. Texas
III. Ohio

A. I only
B. I and II only
C. II, III and IV only
D. I, II, III and IV

165. Which of the following statements is(are) true regarding civil liabilities when a sale violates provisions of the Uniform Securities Act?

I. A buyer may not sue for compensation later than three years after the sale.
II. A rescission offer must include interest.
III. A rescission offer must be at a current price.

A. I only
B. I and II only
C. II only
D. I, II and III

166. Registration statements are effective

A. for a period of time determined by the administrator for each issue
B. for one year from the effective date
C. for one year from the date of issue
D. until the next registration statement is filed

167. Which of the following statements are true regarding registration of securities by coordination?

    I. The cooling-off period for the SEC is 20 days.
    II. The registration statement must be on file with the state administrator for 10 days.
    III. The registration becomes effective in the state only after the state's cooling-off period.
    IV. The registration becomes effective at the state level in conjunction with the SEC if the administrator has not entered an order to deny it.

    A. I, II and IV only
    B. II and III only
    C. III and IV only
    D. I, II, III and IV

168. All of the following are exempt securities EXCEPT

    I. U.S. government securities
    II. unsolicited transactions
    III. transactions between issuers and underwriters
    IV. securities of credit unions

    A. I, II and IV
    B. I and IV
    C. II and III
    D. IV

169. An agent finds out from his uncle, an office manager at Microscam, that Microscam is going to acquire Datawaq. The agent should

    A. call all of his customers and tell them to buy Datawaq
    B. call all of his customers and tell them to sell short Microscam
    C. inform his supervisor or principal
    D. buy the stock in his mother's account

170. An agent has a good customer with a margin account. The customer informs the agent that he is taking a business trip for a month. He tells the agent to handle the account. While the customer is gone, the stock market goes down and the customer receives a margin call for $1,000. The agent should

    A. pay the $1,000 on behalf of his good customer and collect at a later date
    B. arrange a loan from a local bank to cover the margin call
    C. sell some securities in the account and use the proceeds to cover the margin call
    D. try to make contact with the customer and, failing that, inform his principal and do nothing until instructed

171. An agent and his sister open a special cash account at the agent's broker-dealer. Both parties contribute $5,000 to the account and purchase $10,000 worth of securities. The agent

    A. can open the account, but cannot share in any profits
    B. can share in the profits to the extent of his proportional contribution with written employer and customer consent
    C. needs only the employer's consent to open the account and can share in the profits
    D. cannot share in any profits

172. An agent gets a phone call from the wife of a customer. The wife wants to sell $25,000 worth of securities and use the proceeds as a down payment on a house. The account is in her husband's name, but she says he told her to sell the securities. The agent knows the couple to be happily married. He should

    A. call the husband immediately and confirm the order
    B. sell as instructed
    C. get permission from his principal
    D. tell the couple that the purchase of a house is a bad investment

173. A customer asks an agent for advice in choosing a balanced mutual fund for an IRA. The agent may state which of the following?

    A. "Last year, ArGood Mutual Fund was up 40 percent. Based on this past performance, I expect the trend to continue, thus making it suitable for an IRA."
    B. "I guarantee that you will make money in ArGood Mutual Fund over a long period of time based on past performance, making it a good investment for an IRA."
    C. "Last year, ArGood Mutual Fund was up 40 percent. However, over the last 10 years, ArGood had both up and down periods. The potential for gain does exist; however, there is no guarantee as to how much gain or loss will take place."
    D. "ArGood Mutual Fund is such a good buy that I will guarantee against any losses personally."

174. The net asset value in NavCo Mutual Fund is $9 per share. Currently, the fund pays $.60 per share in annual dividends and $2 in capital gains distributions. The projections for the next year are $.75 per share in annual dividends and $2.50 per share in capital gains distributions. The agent could state which of the following to the customer?

    A. "Currently, the NavCo Mutual Fund has paid $.60 per share in dividends and guarantees to pay $.75 per share this year."
    B. "The current yield in NavCo Mutual Fund is 6.7 percent. However, the research report on NavCo Mutual Fund projects the possibility of a higher current yield next year."
    C. 'The fund is yielding 29 percent currently, and the expectation is for a higher rate of return for next year."
    D. "The projected yield on the fund this year would be in the neighborhood of 36 percent."

175. A customer is upset with her agent for not servicing her account properly and sends him a complaint letter about his actions. The agent should

    A. call the customer and apologize, promising to do a better job
    B. tell the customer he is willing to make rescission
    C. do nothing and hope that he doesn't hear any more about it
    D. bring the customer complaint to his employer immediately

176. Which of the following would NOT be considered a market manipulation?

    A. Three market markers intentionally start buying and selling the same security simultaneously in their own accounts.
    B. A specialist buys and sells stock for his own account.
    C. A principal in a broker-dealer allows a rumor to leak out that Kelptek is going to acquire Consolidated Codfish. After a few days, the broker-dealer sells short Consolidated Codfish for its own account.
    D. All of the above are examples of market manipulation.

177. In order to get a sale of $10,000 worth of bonds, an agent promises to balance a customer's checkbook each month for as long as the customer remains an account of his, even though the agent is in line for a promotion and an office transfer. This is considered a(n)

    A. acceptable practice
    B. unacceptable practice
    C. practice that is not a violation; however, it is not a wise practice
    D. acceptable practice if it is in accordance with house rules

178. According to the Uniform Securities Act, which of the following statements regarding state registration of securities is true?

    A. Registration by filing is effective when so ordered by the administrator.
    B. Registration by coordination is effective concurrently with federal registration.
    C. Registration by qualification is effective after 30 days.
    D. Registration by coordination is effective when so ordered by the administrator.

179. All of the following are examples of prohibited sales practices EXCEPT

    A. buying on one exchange and selling on another
    B. withholding a material fact from the buyer
    C. buying and selling intentionally to show market activity
    D. giving a phony quote

180. A customer has a discretionary account. The objective of the account is current income. The agent purchases a speculative growth stock. This is considered a(n)

    A. wash sale
    B. unauthorized transaction
    C. acceptable transaction
    D. matching activity

181. Under the Uniform Securities Act, if an investment adviser has custody of customer funds and securities, how often must the adviser send the customer a statement of account activity?

    A. Annually
    B. Quarterly
    C. Monthly
    D. With every transaction

182. Which of the following are examples of fraudulent practices?

    I. Matched orders
    II. Phony quotes
    III. Material misrepresentations
    IV. Wash sales

    A. I and II only
    B. I, II and III only
    C. III and IV only
    D. I, II, III and IV

183. Which of the following is an example of market manipulation?

    A. Creating the illusion of active trading
    B. Buying on one exchange and selling on another
    C. Fictitious quotes to customers
    D. Transactions in excess of customers' financial capabilities

184. As defined in the Uniform Securities Act, which of the following is NOT considered a security?

    A. Fixed annuity
    B. Stock option
    C. Limited partnership unit
    D. Commodity option

185. An agent fails to state facts in which a prudent investor would be interested. This action

    A. is fraudulent under the USA for nonexempt securities only
    B. is fraudulent under the USA for exempt securities only
    C. is fraudulent under the USA for both exempt and nonexempt securities
    D. does not constitute fraud if there was no willful intent to omit the information

186. A customer living in one state receives a phone call from an agent in another state. A transaction between the two occurs in yet another state. Under whose jurisdiction does the transaction fall?

    A. Administrator of the state in which the customer lives
    B. Administrator of the state in which the agent's office is located
    C. Administrator of the state in which the transaction took place
    D. Administrators of all three states involved

187. An agent who willfully violated state securities law is subject to which of the following?

    I. Civil liabilities
    II. Criminal penalties
    III. Denial, suspension or revocation of registration as an agent by the administrator

    A. I only
    B. I and II only
    C. III only
    D. I, II and III

188. A person who sells securities in violation of state securities laws is civilly liable for which of the following?

    I. Principal
    II. Interest
    III. Court costs
    IV. Attorney's fees

    A. I, II and IV only
    B. I and III only
    C. II, III and IV only
    D. I, II, III and IV

189. An agent's license could be revoked if he were

    A. convicted of a securities-related misdemeanor
    B. declared insolvent
    C. either convicted of a securities-related misdemeanor or declared insolvent
    D. Once issued, an agent's license cannot be revoked.

190. Which of the following would subject an agent to a possible denial of registration?

    I. Engagement in fraud in selling to an insurance company
    II. Conviction of a security misdemeanor eight years ago
    III. Insolvency
    IV. Failure to pay filing fees

    A. I only
    B. I, II and III only
    C. II, III and IV only
    D. I, II, III and IV

191. Which of the following is a securities information processor?

    A. Television channel that provides up-to-the-minute information on the current prices of specific stocks
    B. Brokerage firm that provides its customers with securities prices on a continuing basis
    C. Provider of a ticker tape service
    D. Daily newspaper that includes a comprehensive financial section, listing prices of both stocks and mutual funds

192. According to the Uniform Securities Act, from which of the following customers may an investment adviser borrow money?

    I. Affiliate of the investment adviser
    II. Broker-dealer
    III. Bank
    IV. Issuer of blue chip stock

    A. I, II and III
    B. I and IV
    C. II and III
    D. III

193. Under the Uniform Securities Act, all of the following persons may provide investment advice incidental to their normal business without requiring registration as an investment adviser EXCEPT a(n)

    A. teacher
    B. economist
    C. lawyer
    D. engineer

194. Under the Uniform Securities Act, all of the following are excluded from the definition of broker-dealer EXCEPT a(n)

    I. investment adviser
    II. bank
    III. issuer
    IV. financial planner

    A. I and III
    B. I and IV
    C. II and III
    D. IV

◆ Answers & Rationale

1. **True**. U.S. government issues are securities.

2. **False**. Fixed annuities (those that pay a guaranteed, unchangeable amount each month) are specifically exempted from the definition of "securities."

3. **True**. The return of variable annuities is tied to the return on the underlying separate account, and because that account is generally invested in securities, the variable annuity is considered a security.

4. **True**. Certificates representing interests in pension and profit-sharing plans are included in the definition of "securities."

5. **False**. A Keogh plan is a retirement plan in which securities can be purchased or placed, but it is not a security itself.

6. **True**. Collateral trust certificates are included in the definition of "securities."

7. **True**. Preorganization certificates are included in the definition of "securities."

8. **False**. A passbook is not transferable and is not a security. Withdrawals may be made only by a person whose signature is on file for that specific account.

9. **True**. Interests in oil and gas drilling programs are included in the definition of "securities."

10. **True**. Interests in real estate condominiums are included in the definition of "securities."

11. **False**. Term policies are specifically exempted from the definition of "securities."

12. **True**. Interests in farmland or animals (racehorses, prize bulls, ostriches and so on) are included in the definition of "securities."

13. **False**. A prospectus is a document that constitutes an offer to sell specific securities. The prospectus itself has no monetary value and is not transferable.

14. **True**. Option contracts for wheat and other commodities (such as corn, natural gas and currencies) are included in the definition of "securities."

15. **True**. Whiskey warehouse receipts represent interests in a security and are included in the definition of "securities."

16. **True**. Evidences of indebtedness (such as an interest in a condominium pool or another type of collateralized note) are included in the definition of "securities."

17. **False**. A money order has a set value and is not an investment that could be transferable for a profit to a third party.

18. **False**. A confirmation of a securities transaction is used to confirm the particulars of the transaction (name of the security, number of shares and so on), but it is not itself a security.

19. **True**. Certificates representing interests in multilevel distributorship or marketing plans are included in the definition of "securities."

20. **True**. Certificates representing interests in merchandise marketing plans are included in the definition of "securities."

21. **True**. Certificates representing interests in oil and gas or mining titles and leases are included in the definition of "securities."

22. **True**. Unincorporated and incorporated investment clubs are included in the broad legal definition of "person."

23. **True**. All national and municipal governments are included in the broad legal definition of "person."

24. **True**. Legal entities such as the State of New York are included in the broad legal definition of "person."

25. **True**. Corporations, partnerships and sole proprietorships are all included in the broad legal definition of "person."

26. **True**. Individual investors are included in the broad legal definition of "person."

27. **True**. A securities brokerage firm, an investment adviser, an issuer and all others in the financial industry are included in the broad legal definition of "person."

28. **False**. Any transaction involving the primary offering of securities is considered an issuer transaction.

29. **True**. Any transactions in the secondary market, such as trades on an exchange, are considered nonissuer transactions.

30. **False**. An initial offering of stock from a corporation is considered an issuer transaction.

31. **True**. Any transactions in the secondary market, such as trades between over-the-counter broker-dealers or market makers, are considered nonissuer transactions.

32. **False**. A person who has not established a place of business in the state and who has a client base consisting exclusively of financial institutions need not register as a broker-dealer.

33. **False**. A person who deals only with other broker-dealers and who has no place of business in a state is not considered a broker-dealer.

34. **False**. A person who deals only with issuers and who has no place of business in a state is not considered a broker-dealer.

35. **False**. A broker-dealer with no place of business in a state is permitted to direct an offer into the state without being registered in the state if it meets certain conditions. The broker-dealer must be registered in another state where it has a place of business, and the offer must be directed to an existing customer who has less than 30 days' temporary residency.

36. **True**. A person (including a retail broker-dealer) who has established a place of business in a state must register as a broker-dealer.

37. **False**. An agent represents a broker-dealer.

38. **True**. Any individual who effects transactions in exempt securities for a broker-dealer is considered an agent. An individual who effects transactions in exempt securities, such as municipal or government securities, for an *issuer* is not considered an agent.

39. **False**. If the person had been effecting the transactions in commercial paper for a broker-dealer rather than an issuer, the individual would be considered an agent.

40. **True**. An agent is an individual person other than a broker-dealer who represents a broker-dealer or an issuer in effecting transactions in securities.

41. **True**. An agent is an individual person other than a broker-dealer who represents a broker-dealer or an issuer in effecting transactions in securities, including common stock.

42. **True**. An individual who effects exempt transactions does not have to register. Transactions with financial institutions are exempt transactions.

43. **True**. The Uniform Securities Act does not distinguish between attempting to effect a transaction and successfully effecting a transaction. If a partner, an officer or a director of a broker-dealer attempts to effect transactions for securi-

ties, she must be registered as an agent in that state.

44. **False**. An individual who effects transactions with an underwriter on behalf of an issuer is not considered an agent.

45. **False**. The securities of a foreign corporation could not be handled legally by a representative of an issuer who is not a registered agent.

46. **True**. A person representing an issuer in a transaction for an exempted security, such as bonds issued by the Canadian government, could handle the transaction legally without registering as an agent.

47. **True**. A person representing an issuer in a transaction for an exempted security, such as the securities issued by banks, savings and loans and trust companies, could handle the transaction legally without registering as an agent.

48. **True**. A person representing an issuer in a transaction for an exempted security, such as commercial paper, could handle the transaction legally without registering as an agent.

49. **False**. Exchange-listed securities of a corporation could not be handled legally by a representative of an issuer who is not a registered agent.

50. **False**. Banks, savings and loans and trust companies are not included in the definition of "investment adviser."

51. **False**. Lawyers, accountants, engineers and other professionals who advise others on investments incidentally to the practice of their own professions are not included in the definition of "investment adviser."

52. **True**. Anyone who engages in the business of giving investment advice for a fee is considered an investment adviser.

53. **True**. Impersonal advisory services include statistical information on specific investments which is made available to a specific group.

54. **False**. The publishers of a general circulation, business and financial newspaper or magazine that does not provide individualized advice are not included in the definition of "investment adviser."

55. **True**. Under the Uniform Securities Act, persons whose investment advice relates solely to exempt securities, such as U.S. government and municipal securities, are included in the definition of "investment adviser."

56. **True**. In addition to the standard exemptions from the definition of "investment adviser," the state administrator may designate any other person as exempt, as he sees fit.

57. **True**. A company that raises capital by issuing shares in itself is considered an issuer of securities.

58. **True**. The Uniform Securities Act does not distinguish between a proposed issue and an actual issue of securities in defining "issuer."

59. **False**. The president is not considered an issuer because it is the corporate person, Kelptek, Inc. that is issuing the securities.

60. **D**.   Nonissuer transactions are any transactions that do not directly benefit an issuer.

61. **D**.   The Uniform Securities Act specifies that the state's administrator (who also may be called the commissioner or secretary) has the authority to enforce the act in that state.

62. **C**.   The security has a backer (such as an insurance company or a parent company) that has guaranteed the payment of principal, interest or dividends.

63. **A.** An offer is made in an attempt to sell. A sale is the binding contract to sell.

64. **D.** Although institutional investors typically trade very large blocks of securities, there is no upper or lower limit placed on the size of their trades.

65. **True.** The administrator in a state may require that broker-dealers seeking registration in that state have and maintain a certain minimum net capital.

66. **True.** An administrator may require a surety bond.

67. **True.** The administrator in a state has the right to require officers or executive officers of a broker-dealer to qualify by written or oral exam.

68. **False.** The agent, the new employer and the former employer all must notify the administrator.

69. **False.** The administrator may require other exams in addition to the Uniform Securities Agent State Law Examination (USASLE) of any reasonably defined class of persons (such as broker-dealers, state-registered investment advisers or representatives).

70. **True.** Licensing begins and ends with employment by a registered broker-dealer. Registration is not transferable and must be canceled and renewed when an agent changes employment.

71. **False.** Only those persons who are officers at the time the broker-dealer is registered and who act in the capacity of agents are registered automatically.

72. **False.** The person must be registered as an agent in any state in which she wishes to transact securities business, even if the securities or the transactions involved in any offer or sale are exempt from registration requirements.

73. **A.** Under the amended act, investment advisers are now exempt from registration in any one state if they solicit less than six clients within the year.

74. **False.** A person whose clients are individuals must be registered as an investment adviser in that state before transacting business.

75. **False.** If a broker-dealer receives special compensation for investment advice, she must be registered as an investment adviser.

76. **False.** A consent to service of process and a filing fee also must be filed to obtain a registration.

77. **True.** The administrator may ask for any information from the broker-dealer that he deems necessary.

78. **False.** Registered broker-dealers and state-registered investment advisers must file regular financial reports with the state administrator.

79. **True.** Broker-dealers and state-registered investment advisers must file with the state administrator a complete business methods proposal. Federally-registered investment advisers must give notice only to state administrators and pay filing fees.

80. **False.** The investment adviser of a registered investment company must register with the SEC only. Recordkeeping and reporting requirements are established by the SEC. State administrators have no jurisdiction over federally registered investment companies.

81. **False.** Under the NSMIA and the USA, registered investment companies are exempt from state registration and reporting requirements.

82. **B.** The National Securities Markets Improvement Act of 1996 defines the SEC's function and responsibilities as well as the state

securities administrators' authority level. Federal law now overrides state law.

83. **C.** In order to register a security by qualification, the issuer must file with the state administrator any registration documents and other information the administrator requires.

84. **A.** A registration by coordination is used when the issuer is registering the offering with the SEC at the same time. Copies of the registration documents filed with the SEC also are filed with the administrator of the state.

85. **B.** Registration by filing and by coordination become effective concurrently with the federal registration.

86. **Nonexempt**

87. **Exempt**

88. **Exempt**

89. **Nonexempt.** The only political subdivisions that are granted exempt status are in Canada.

90. **Exempt**

91. **Exempt**

92. **Exempt**

93. **Exempt**

94. **Nonexempt**

95. **Exempt**

96. **Exempt.** This corporation is a common carrier subject to the ICC.

97. **Nonexempt.** Securities listed on a U.S. securities exchange are exempt.

98. **Exempt**

99. **Exempt** or **nonexempt.** Some Nasdaq securities are exempt, and others are not.

100. **Nonexempt**

101. **False.** An agent must be registered to make solicitations in a state, whether the security is exempt or nonexempt. For example, to sell municipals in another state, the agent must be registered in that state.

102. **True.** Registration is not required if the securities are not distributed by means of public offering.

103. **True**

104. **False.** The key word is "solicit." One cannot solicit orders and then claim they were unsolicited.

105. **False.** The number of nonexempt unregistered secondary (nonissuer) transactions that can be made varies from state to state. For example, one state might permit only one transaction in any one 12-month period. Do not confuse this regulation with the rules governing private placements, which limit offerings to no more than 10 nonaccredited investors in any 12-month period. Private placements are primary (issuer) transactions.

106. **True**

107. **True**

108. **True.** The burden of proof that a transaction is unsolicited lies with the agent.

109. **True.** Executors are fiduciaries; therefore, the transactions are exempt.

110. **True.** Under the USA, no commissions may be paid for soliciting nonaccredited investors.

111. **False**. A private placement is an exempt transaction of nonexempt securities.

112. **Unlawful.** Implying that the $1 year-end special dividend was part of a normal dividend-paying procedure is misleading.

113. **Unlawful.** The earnings have increased at the rate of 75 percent for the last two years (100 percent and 50 percent). However, because this limited information does not tell the complete story of recent years' earnings, it is misleading.

114. **Unlawful.** The three percentages do average out to a 33 1/3 percent increase in earnings, but the statement is materially misleading. The 100 percent increase in the middle year simply offsets the 50 percent decrease of the previous year. This is a good example of the misuse of numbers that constitutes fraud.

115. **Unlawful.** This calculation is misleading because it does not inform the client of the decline that occurred in earnings per share. Leaving out material information constitutes fraud.

116. **Lawful.** Clearly, the agent is attempting to cover the material facts when discussing the earnings per share. No fraud is involved here.

117. **Unlawful.** Stock offerings bring in more capital. The additional capital usually produces additional earnings, so examining net earnings without offering a per-share comparison is misleading and fraudulent.

118. **Unlawful.** This agent should have pointed out that the Exchange listing requirements are, in many cases, quantitative, not qualitative. Acceptance for listing by the New York Stock Exchange does not necessarily reduce the risk of loss to the client. The agent's statement is misleading and, therefore, prohibited.

119. **Unlawful.** An agent's telling clients that exchange listing of a security is anticipated when he has no knowledge of the truth of such a statement is prohibited.

120. **Unlawful.** An execution price of 14 3/4 constitutes a markup of a quarter of a point. The agent has indicated there would be no markup.

121. **Unlawful.** Neither the SEC nor the state approves the accuracy or the adequacy of information regarding a new issue.

122. **Unlawful.** The agent misrepresents the status of the account to the client. He also induces the client to make a transaction that might not be suitable at that time.

123. **Unlawful.** An agent's promising to perform certain services on a client's behalf when he has no intent to perform those services is a prohibited activity.

124. **Unlawful.** With rare exception, this action constitutes promising to perform certain services on a client's behalf without any intent to perform those services or without being properly qualified to perform those services.

125. **Unlawful.** Misrepresenting to clients the status of their accounts is prohibited.

126. **Unlawful.** Obviously, an agent cannot give every fact in his sales presentation, but he must give all material facts.

127. **Unlawful.** The agent failed to describe sufficiently the important facts and risks concerning a transaction or set of transactions.

128. **Lawful.** Because the agent has material nonpublic information, he is considered an insider and cannot take advantage of the information. On the other hand, this agent's continuing to recommend the stock would not be in the best interest of his clients and would mean he would have to withhold material facts.

129. **Unlawful.** An agent must not take advantage of inside information.

130. **Unlawful.** This agent failed to make a reasonable inquiry as to the customer's needs and

objectives. Refusing to do business may be the only good business practice available to an agent in certain situations.

131. **Unlawful.** This action constitutes recommending security transactions to clients without regard to their individual financial situations. It is highly unlikely that shares of stock in a new company would be a suitable investment for every one of any agent's clients.

132. **Unlawful.** The agent either did not make a reasonable inquiry as to the customer's financial situation or he induced a transaction that was excessive in size in relation to the customer's financial resources. Either action is prohibited.

133. **Unlawful.** The agent is recommending the purchase of a security without reasonable grounds for the recommendation. The agent is probably also guilty of recommending security transactions without regard to clients' individual financial situations or investment objectives.

134. **Unlawful.** This action is called *churning* and is prohibited.

135. **Unlawful.** This action constitutes recommending the purchase of a security without reasonable grounds for the recommendation.

136. **Lawful.** This action is not fraudulent or prohibited.

137. **Lawful.** The agent is making a recommendation based on reasonable grounds.

138. **Unlawful.** Accepting orders on behalf of customers from individuals other than the customers without first obtaining third-party trading authority is a prohibited business practice.

139. **Unlawful.** Failing to inform a client that certain transactions involve larger than ordinary commissions, taxes or other costs is prohibited.

140. **Unlawful.** Borrowing money or securities from a client is a prohibited business practice.

141. **Unlawful.** The agent cannot commingle his funds with a client's funds.

142. **Unlawful.** Deliberately failing to follow a customer's instructions is prohibited.

143. **Unlawful.** The agent effected a transaction on behalf of a customer without the specific authority to do so.

144. **Unlawful.** Effecting transactions with a client not recorded on the regular books or records of the agent's employing broker-dealer is not allowed, unless those transactions are authorized in writing by the broker-dealer before the execution of the transactions.

145. **Unlawful.** The agent has failed to bring a client's written complaints to the attention of his employing broker-dealer.

146. **Unlawful.** The agent failed to inform the client that certain transactions involve higher than ordinary commissions, taxes or other costs.

147. **Unlawful.** Assuring clients that they will make a profit is a prohibited practice. Besides, it is all too possible to lose money (interest rate risk) on fixed-income securities when interest rates go up.

148. **Unlawful.** This transaction is a wash sale, which may reasonably be expected to distort the trading in a security. This prohibited activity is sometimes referred to as *painting the tape*. Do not confuse this activity with an arbitrage transaction, which is legal. (An arbitrage transaction is the simultaneous purchase and sale of the same security on different exchanges to take advantage of a price difference.)

149. **Unlawful.** Soliciting orders for unregistered nonexempt securities is illegal whether or not this effort results in an order.

150. **No.** Written consent is required from the client.

151. **No**. Notification is necessary when the adviser is a participant in a partnership, but not when the adviser is a participant in a corporation.

152. **No**

153. **Yes**

154. **No.** An investment adviser must provide notice to the administrator if he has or may have custody of customer funds or securities.

155. **Yes.** If an adviser has (or may have in the future) custody of customer funds or securities, the administrator must be notified.

156. **C.** Answers A and D are incorrect because neither choice I nor choice III by itself justifies an action for denial.

157. **B.** Choices I and II would be grounds for the suspension of an agent's registration by the state administrator.

158. **True**

159. **True**

160. **False**

161. **False**

162. **False**. The administrator cannot use lack of experience alone to determine qualification.

163. **A.** The seller can offer to buy back the security at the purchase price plus an interest rate set by the state administrator.

164. **B.** The offer was made from Illinois to a person in California, and so the state administrators of both states would have jurisdiction. The state from which payment was mailed and the state in which the checking account or money-market fund is based are unimportant.

165. **B.** Rescission must occur by the earlier of two years after the discovery of the facts or three years after the occurrence.

166. **B.** Registration statements are effective for one year from the effective date.

167. **A.** The federal 1933 securities act requires that securities offered to the public be registered with the SEC. The registration statement becomes effective on the 20th calendar day following the date the statement is received by the SEC (assuming the SEC does not find any deficiencies or misrepresentations). During the 20-day cooling-off period between the filing date and the effective date, indications of interest from the public for shares may be taken. When the registration becomes effective, shares in the new issue may be reconfirmed and actual orders taken. Note that on the federal level, the registration must be on file with the SEC for 20 days, while on the state level it must be on file with the administrator for 10 days.

168. **C.** Take care to distinguish between an exempt security and an exempt transaction.

169. **C.** Making recommendations on the basis of material inside information is a fraudulent or deceitful business practice.

170. **D.** For margin accounts falling below the minimum maintenance amount required, and if the customer cannot be reached, the agent should inform his principal, who will then determine which and how many securities must be sold to maintain the margin requirement as set by Regulation T. The agent may not take further action or execute any transactions without a written trading authorization.

171. **B.** The agent may share in proportion to his contribution, assuming he has written consent of the broker-dealer and the customer.

172. **A.** The agent may accept orders only from the customer, unless third-party trading authorization has been obtained.

173. **C.** The agent has the responsibility to describe sufficiently the risks and to state all important facts. Offering a guarantee is obviously misleading.

174. **B.** Misrepresenting yields is clearly fraudulent.

175. **D.** Failure to bring customers' written complaints to the attention of the agent's broker-dealer is prohibited.

176. **B.** The function of the specialist normally is to act as a broker for orders left with him by other members and to act as a dealer in buying and selling for his own account.

177. **B.** An agent may not make promises that probably cannot be kept.

178. **B.** Coordination is frequently used to register a security simultaneously under the Securities Act of 1933 and in a state. If the security's federal registration is pending and the administrator has received all of the required material, the two registrations can be declared effective at the same time.

179. **A.** Buying on one exchange and selling on another is a perfectly acceptable market arbitrage.

180. **B.** The customer authorized the agent to buy income-producing securities only. Wash sale and matching activity refer to creating the impression of activity in the stock by buying and selling the same stock at the same price without a change in beneficial ownership. These activities may cause others to buy or sell the security.

181. **B.** An investment adviser in possession of customer assets must send a statement to the customer every three months; the statement must list the securities held by the adviser and must show all transactions in the account since the last statement date.

182. **D.** All of the activities listed are fraudulent practices.

183. **A.** Creating the illusion of trading activity is a manipulation of the market. Arbitrage (choice B) is not market manipulation. Giving fictitious quotes is prohibited because they are untrue statements; however, it is not market manipulation. Trades that are too large for a customer also are prohibited because they are not suitable, but they are not considered market manipulation.

184. **A.** A fixed annuity is an insurance contract that cannot be traded for value. Commodity options (although not the underlying futures contracts) and stock options are considered securities, as are interests purchased in a limited partnership enterprise.

185. **C.** The omission of a material fact in the sale, purchase or offer of a security is fraudulent. This applies whether the security being offered is exempt or nonexempt.

186. **D.** The Uniform Securities Act gives the state administrator jurisdiction over offers to buy or sell when the offers originate in the administrator's state or are directed to or accepted in that state.

187. **D.** Violations of securities laws are subject to criminal penalties, civil liabilities and denial, suspension or revocation of registration.

188. **D.** The person illegally selling the securities is liable for the purchase price of the securities plus interest from the date of purchase, costs and reasonable attorney's fees.

189. **C.** If you missed this, review the list in the text on offenses leading to denial, suspension or revocation of registration.

190. **D.** Fraud, conviction of a felony or misdemeanor involving a security and insolvency are grounds for denial.

191. **C.** A provider of a ticker tape service is included in the definition of a securities information processor; all of the other choices are excluded from the definition.

192. **A.**   An investment adviser may not borrow money from a customer unless the customer is an affiliate of the investment adviser, a broker-dealer, or a bank or another institution in the business of lending money.

193. **B.**   The Uniform Securities Act exempts from registration teachers, engineers, lawyers and accountants providing investment advice that is incidental to the performance of their normal business. Economists are not granted an exemption under the act.

194. **B.**   The USA excludes issuers and banks from the definition of broker-dealer, as well as agents. Investment advisers and financial planners are not granted exclusions from the definition.

6 ◆ Uniform Securities Act Exam One

1. As defined in the Uniform Securities Act, which of the following is NOT a security?

   A. Interest in a real estate condominium
   B. Commercial paper issued with an eight-month maturity
   C. Variable annuity
   D. $100,000 whole life insurance policy

2. Which of the following persons is defined as an agent by the Uniform Securities Act?

   A. Silent partner
   B. Secretary of a sales manager
   C. Clerk who is authorized to take orders
   D. Executive who does not solicit or transact business

3. As defined in the Uniform Securities Act, which of the following are considered securities?

   I. Commodity option contract
   II. Treasury stock
   III. Keogh plan

   A. I and II only
   B. I and III only
   C. II and III only
   D. I, II and III

4. According to the Uniform Securities Act, an investment adviser is all of the following EXCEPT a

   I. broker who charges for investment advice
   II. publisher of a financial newspaper
   III. person who sells security analysis
   IV. CPA who charges for constructing a portfolio of tax-sheltered investments

   A. I and II
   B. II and III
   C. II and IV
   D. III and IV

5. Interests in which of the following are considered securities under the Uniform Securities Act?

   I. Merchandising marketing scheme
   II. Multilevel distributorship arrangement
   III. Oil and gas drilling program

   A. I and II only
   B. I and III only
   C. II and III only
   D. I, II and III

6. Under the Uniform Securities Act, an individual is required to register as an "agent" if she represents an issuer in which of the following transactions?

   A. Sale of six-month commercial paper
   B. Sale of Canadian corporation's common stock
   C. Transaction with an underwriter
   D. Transaction in municipal securities

7. Under the Uniform Securities Act, the definition of "issuer" includes which of the following?

   A. Seller in a transaction on the floor of an exchange
   B. Officer or director of a company that is offering new shares to the public
   C. Person proposing to issue a security
   D. Market maker for a new issue

8. Under the Uniform Securities Act, the definition of "broker-dealer" includes a(n)

   A. person in the business of making trades in his own account or for the accounts of others
   B. agent handling principal transactions
   C. trust company when executing transactions in accounts in which it does NOT act in a fiduciary capacity
   D. authorized representative of the issuer

9. According to the Uniform Securities Act, a sale is a(n)

   A. attempt to transfer ownership of a security
   B. solicitation of an offer to buy
   C. contract to transfer ownership of a security for value
   D. offer equivalent contract

10. Under the Uniform Securities Act, all of the following are considered securities EXCEPT

    A. warehouse receipts
    B. fixed-annuity contracts
    C. preorganization certificates
    D. commercial paper

11. An employee of a large publicly held company effects transactions with existing employees for the purchase of company debentures. Under the Uniform Securities Act, which of the following statements is true?

    A. He must register as an agent of the issuer.
    B. He never need register as an agent of the issuer.
    C. He may receive commissions without registration.
    D. He must register as an agent if he will receive commissions or remuneration, directly or indirectly.

12. According to the Uniform Securities Act, which of the following is NOT considered a person?

    A. Custodian
    B. Minor
    C. Municipality
    D. Corporation

13. Under the Uniform Securities Act, a person who has passed the Uniform Securities Agent State Law Examination but whose license has not yet been issued can participate in which of the following activities?

    A. Prospecting in person
    B. Prospecting by mail
    C. Accepting unsolicited orders
    D. None of the above

14. According to the Uniform Securities Act, a consent to service of process must accompany which of the following?

    I. Agent's registration application
    II. Civil complaint against a broker-dealer
    III. Broker-dealer's initial registration application

    A. I only
    B. I and III only
    C. II and III only
    D. I, II and III

15. An agent representing a broker-dealer lives in one state and would like to do business in another state. Under the Uniform Securities Act, which of the following statements is true?

    A. No registration is necessary in the other state as long as the agent's activities are limited exclusively to effecting transactions in certain exempted securities.
    B. No registration is necessary if no commission or other remuneration is paid or given directly or indirectly.
    C. If the agent is a partner, an officer or a director and held that position at the time the broker-dealer was registered, the individual need not register separately.
    D. Registration is required only if an offer is directed, accepted and paid for in that state.

16. Persons who have less than $25,000,000 in assets under management must register at what level?

    A. Federal
    B. State
    C. Both federal and state
    D. Neither federal nor state

17. According to the Uniform Securities Act, which of the following may be required by an administrator prior to issuing an agent's license?

    A. Oral or written examination or both
    B. Completed application or evidence of a completed and current registration with the SEC or an SRO
    C. Consent to service of process
    D. All of the above

18. Under the Uniform Securities Act, for what period of time is a broker-dealer's agent's license in effect?

    A. It depends on the renewal dates in the various states.
    B. Until December 31st unless renewed
    C. Until withdrawn by the agent or revoked by the administrator
    D. Length of the agent's employment by all broker-dealers

19. According to the Uniform Securities Act, which of the following is responsible for notifying the administrator when an agent changes his place of employment?

    A. Agent
    B. Former employer
    C. New employer
    D. The agent, the former employer and the new employer

20. Which of the following statements is true regarding an agent's license issued under the Uniform Securities Act?

    A. Upon issuance, it is valid for a predetermined length of time that varies by state.
    B. It is valid immediately after the agent passes an examination.
    C. It is not valid if the agent terminates employment with a broker-dealer.
    D. It is valid for 30 days after termination of employment with a broker-dealer if new employment is pending.

21. Under the Uniform Securities Act, which of the following types of transactions can be entered into legally with unregistered nonexempt securities?

   A. Public offering
   B. Private placement
   C. Rights offering
   D. Offering to employees of the issuer

22. Which of the following securities is(are) exempt from the registration provisions of the Uniform Securities Act?

   I. Issue of a savings and loan association
   II. General obligation municipal bond
   III. Bond issued by a company that has common stock listed on the American Stock Exchange

   A. I only
   B. II only
   C. II and III only
   D. I, II and III

23. Which of the following activities would violate the Uniform Securities Act?

   I. Buying and selling the same stock on the same day on different exchanges
   II. Offering shares of an unregistered nonexempt security to customers
   III. Offering a Canadian government bond to a resident of a state in which the agent of a broker-dealer is not registered

   A. I only
   B. II only
   C. II and III only
   D. I, II and III

24. Which of the following exemptions under the Uniform Securities Act applies to the sale of securities to institutions that are regarded as professional investors?

   A. Blue chip exemption
   B. Manual exemption
   C. Exempt transaction
   D. Exempt security

25. Which of the following statements is true regarding the antifraud provisions of the Uniform Securities Act?

   A. The only securities exempt from the provisions are those regulated by federal authority.
   B. The only exempt securities are those issued by national governments or political subdivisions of countries that maintain diplomatic relations with the United States.
   C. The only exempt securities are those that are properly registered under blue-sky laws.
   D. No securities are exempt from the antifraud provisions of the act.

26. The Uniform Securities Act prohibits which of the following?

   I. Agents exercising discretion in discretionary accounts
   II. Charging larger than ordinary commissions on certain transactions
   III. Soliciting orders for unregistered nonexempt securities

   A. I only
   B. II and III only
   C. III only
   D. I, II and III

27. An agent is asked by a customer to open an account and buy stock for the customer's spouse. According to the Uniform Securities Act, which of the following statements about this action is true?

   A. The agent could be liable if the stock declines in value.
   B. This practice is ordinary and acceptable.
   C. This action is prohibited unless the spouse signs a trading authorization.
   D. This action is prohibited unless the customer signs a trading authorization on behalf of his spouse.

28. A customer who wishes to retire in three years informs his agent that he wants to use the equity in his house to make enough money in the market to fund his retirement. According to the Uniform Securities Act, the agent should

    A. help meet the customer's needs by constructing a high-quality, growth-oriented portfolio
    B. urge the customer to reconsider because the time allotted is not consistent with his means
    C. suggest that the customer invest in an ultraconservative portfolio of municipal bonds
    D. invest the money in stocks because of their unlimited potential

29. An agent hears that the chairman of a large manufacturing firm may be ousted because of erratic social behavior. The agent decides to call all of his customers who own shares of the manufacturing corporation and tell them to liquidate their positions. Under the Uniform Securities Act, which of the following statements is true?

    A. The agent may have made an error as to the effect of the rumor, so he should wait until he has a better feel for the situation.
    B. This action is based on material inside information, so he must inform all of his customers of this fact.
    C. This action constitutes a prohibited use of rumor to induce a purchase or sale.
    D. This action is legal and legitimate as long as the agent limits the exposure to 12 customers or fewer.

30. An agent hears material inside information regarding a company that is publicly held. Which of the following actions would NOT violate the Uniform Securities Act?

    A. Soliciting orders based on this information
    B. Trading for the agent's personal account based on this information
    C. Discussing the situation with a superior or compliance officer in the agent's firm
    D. Discussing the information at a seminar, but not making an investment recommendation

31. Under the Uniform Securities Act, which of the following may have custody of customer funds?

    I. Investment adviser who maintains $35,000 net worth
    II. Investment adviser who maintains $35,000 surety bond
    III. Broker-dealer who maintains $10,000 surety bond
    IV. Broker-dealer in compliance with SEC net capital rules

    A. I and III
    B. I and IV
    C. I, II and IV
    D. III and IV

32. According to the Uniform Securities Act, which of the following would be an unlawful activity for an investment adviser?

    A. Entering into an investment advisory contract that does not mention the compensation arrangements
    B. Taking custody of a customer's securities or funds without notifying the administrator, even though the administrator has no rule that prohibits such custody
    C. Entering into an investment advisory contract that provides specifically for compensation based on a share of capital appreciation of the customer's funds
    D. All of the above

33. Which of the following actions would NOT be considered unlawful under the Uniform Securities Act?

    A. An agent makes an untrue statement of a material fact
    B. An agent omits a material fact because she knew she did not have time to cover everything in a short presentation
    C. An agent deliberately fails to follow a customer's instructions
    D. An agent actively solicits orders in unregistered exempt securities

34. The Uniform Securities Act permits excessive trading activity that generates high commissions and low returns in a customer's account

    A. in discretionary accounts
    B. with written permission of the customer
    C. when it is consistent with the customer's needs
    D. under no circumstances

35. Under the Uniform Securities Act, which of the following statements is true regarding the use of material facts?

    A. To omit them is fraudulent and unethical.
    B. Because all material facts cannot be presented, it is up to the sales rep to decide which to use.
    C. Restrictions apply only to sales, not solicitations.
    D. The agent is the final arbiter on what is material and what is not.

36. Persons with $5,000,000 or less under management who act in an advisory capacity in states that do not require registration must do which of the following?

    A. Register with the SEC.
    B. Register with the NASD.
    C. Pass the Series 7 General Securities Representative Examination.
    D. Pass the Series 65 Uniform Investment Adviser Law Examination.

37. An agent receives a letter from an irate customer. This letter is the fourth in the last four months and is very abusive. The agent decides against a reply, and discards the letter. Under the Uniform Securities Act, which of the following statements is correct?

    A. The agent is entitled to decide how to handle such situations.
    B. The administrator may, by rule, dictate how this should be handled.
    C. All material complaints must be forwarded to the administrator.
    D. The agent's behavior is prohibited. He must forward all written complaints to his employer.

38. Which of the following are considered investment adviser representatives (supervised persons) under the Uniform Securities Act?

    I. Vice-president of the firm
    II. Temporary employee hired to solicit clients
    III. Employee who performs only clerical tasks
    IV. Employee who supervises the management of customer accounts

    A. I only
    B. I, II and IV only
    C. III and IV only
    D. I, II, III and IV

39. According to the Uniform Securities Act, to determine whether an investment adviser is trading excessively in a customer's account, regulators examine whether the

    A. adviser received compensation for the trades
    B. transactions matched the investor's objectives
    C. customer approved the transactions in writing
    D. adviser acted as a principal or an agent

40. Under the Uniform Securities Act, which of the following statements is true of an agent who deliberately gives a fictitious quote to a customer?

    A. He is guilty of a felony.
    B. He has committed a fraudulent and misleading act.
    C. He must execute at that price.
    D. He is committed to selling or buying 100 shares at that price.

41. State securities administrators are required to enforce which of the following with respect to investment advisers who practice within their state?

    A. Rules of Fair Practice
    B. Conduct Rules
    C. Antifraud regulations
    D. Fraud regulations

42. Which of the following is a fraudulent or prohibited activity under the Uniform Securities Act?

    A. Using the dividends paid in the last 12 months to determine the current yield of a common stock
    B. Implying that registration of a security means approval of the security
    C. Selling common stock to a customer with income objectives
    D. Stating that zero-coupon bonds pay no current interest

43. Which of the following practices violates the Uniform Securities Act?

    A. Deliberately not charging a commission
    B. Failing to charge a markup
    C. Failing to state every fact
    D. Failing to follow a customer's instructions

44. An investment adviser ignores a state administrator's subpoena of records. Under the Uniform Securities Act, the adviser may be subject to

    A. a court injunction
    B. a registration revocation
    C. a probationary period
    D. all of the above

45. Under the Uniform Securities Act, the state administrator may revoke or deny an investment adviser's registration for which of the following reasons?

    A. Conviction for a securities felony 15 years ago
    B. Conviction for a securities misdemeanor 15 years ago
    C. Violation of another state's securities law five years ago
    D. Lack of experience as an investment adviser

46. Which of the following statements regarding licensing and registration under the Uniform Securities Act is(are) true?

    I. When an agent's license is suspended, the broker-dealer's also is suspended.
    II. When a broker-dealer's license is suspended, the agent's registration is suspended.
    III. The administrator may suspend or revoke registrations whenever the public good is the sole consideration.
    IV. If a principal's license is suspended, the broker-dealer's license is suspended.

    A. I and II
    B. II and III
    C. II and IV
    D. III and IV

47. If it is in the public interest to do so, the Uniform Securities Act provides that the state administrator may deny the registration of a person for all of the following reasons EXCEPT

    A. the applicant is not qualified owing to lack of experience
    B. a willful violation of the Uniform Securities Act has taken place
    C. the applicant is financially insolvent
    D. the applicant is temporarily enjoined from engaging in the securities business

48. According to the Uniform Securities Act, which of the following would rectify an inadvertent sale of an unregistered nonexempt security?

    I. Offering to buy the security back from the customer
    II. Asking the customer to sign a customer agreement
    III. Registering the stock by notification
    IV. Offering to pay interest as set by the administrator, less income paid, from the date the security was purchased

    A. I and III only
    B. I and IV only
    C. II and III only
    D. I, II, III and IV

49. Which of the following statements is true regarding a state administrator's authority under the Uniform Securities Act?

    A. The administrator has authority over any transaction made in his state.
    B. The administrator may criminally prosecute an agent.
    C. The administrator may suspend an agent's license based solely on the public good doctrine.
    D. The administrator must determine the state from which payment is made and to which securities are delivered.

50. An agent in Alabama directs a solicitation to a customer who lives in Connecticut while the customer is temporarily in Indiana. The customer does not accept the offer until he arrives back in Connecticut. According to the Uniform Securities Act, the administrators of which states have jurisdiction?

    A. Alabama and Connecticut
    B. Alabama and Indiana
    C. Indiana and Connecticut
    D. Alabama, Connecticut and Indiana

◆ Answers & Rationale

1. **D.** "Security" can be defined as any piece of paper that can be traded for value. An investment is considered a security if a person invests her money in a common enterprise with the expectation of profit from the managerial efforts of a third party. Insurance policies and fixed annuities are not considered securities.
(Page 4)

2. **C.** Anyone who solicits or receives an order while representing a broker-dealer is an agent. (Page 2)

3. **A.** An IRA or a Keogh plan is a vehicle for an investment, not a security itself. Note that a commodity option contract is considered a security, while a commodity futures contract is not a security. (Page 4)

4. **C.** Investment advisers are persons in the business of selling investment advice. Professionals such as lawyers, accountants and teachers whose performance is incidental to the practice of their profession are not considered investment advisers. (Page 20)

5. **D.** All of the investments mentioned fall into the definition of "security." (Page 4)

6. **B.** An individual is not considered an agent when representing an issuer in such securities as municipal securities, Canadian government securities or commercial paper maturing in 270 days or less. Also, an individual is not considered an agent when representing an issuer in exempt transactions, such as between the issuer and underwriter. However, an individual representing a Canadian issuer of common stock is included in the Uniform Securities Act's definition of "agent." (Page 12)

7. **C.** The term "issuer" includes any person who issues or proposes to issue any security.
(Page 3)

8. **A.** "Broker-dealer" is defined as any individual or firm in the business of making trades in its own account or for the accounts of others.
(Page 2)

9. **C.** "Sale" is defined as every contract to sell a security or an interest in a security, including a security given as a bonus with the purchase of another security, or a gift of assessable stock. "Offer to sell" is defined as an attempt to solicit a purchase or sale in a security. (Page 3)

10. **B.** Fixed annuities are not considered securities. (Page 4)

11. **D.** An individual is not considered an agent when effecting transactions with an issuer's employees only if no commission is paid.
(Page 12)

12. **B.** Minors cannot enter into contracts and are therefore not considered legal persons.
(Page 20)

13. **D.** A person who has passed the exam cannot transact business until the state administrator grants registration, which normally is on the 30th day after the application is filed.
(Page 13)

14. **B.** A broker-dealer, an agent or a state-registered investment adviser may obtain registration by filing an application and a consent to service of process with the administrator. The consent to service of process gives the administrator the irrevocable right to process legal complaints against the applicant. Federally registered advisers must give notice only and pay filing fees in the states in which they conduct business.
(Page 13)

15. **C.** Both the broker-dealer and the agent must be registered in the state where business is to be transacted, even if the securities or the transactions are exempt from registration. At the time the broker-dealer is registered, officers of the firm who act as agents will be registered automatically as agents. (Page 11)

16.   **B.**   Persons who have less than $25 million in assets under management must register on a state basis. These advisers will be referred to as "state-registered" investment advisers.   (Page 23)

17.   **D.**   As a condition of registration, the state administrator may require that an agent pass a written or an oral examination or both. Most states also may require applicants, their firms or both to provide a completed application and a consent to service of process.   (Page 13)

18.   **B.**   Registrations expire on December 31st of each year unless renewed.   (Page 16)

19.   **D.**   All three parties must notify the administrator.   (Page 14)

20.   **C.**   After passing the exam, the agent must be granted registration by the state administrator. If the administrator does not deny registration, it becomes effective 30 days following the application.   (Page 13)

21.   **B.**   Private placements involve the sale of nonexempt securities to qualified public investors. Private placement transactions are exempt from registration. The Uniform Securities Act stipulates that no more than 10 nonaccredited investors receive offers in any 12-month period; that the purchase be made for the purpose of investment; and that no commissions be paid for solicitation of non-institutional buyers.   (Page 62)

22.   **D.**   Each of the securities listed is exempt from registration under the Uniform Securities Act.   (Page 59)

23.   **C.**   Buying a security on one exchange and selling it on another is a proper market arbitrage. Broker-dealers and agents must be registered in each state where offers or sales occur. Also, every security must be registered unless it is an exempt security or an exempt transaction.   (Page 69)

24.   **C.**   The Uniform Securities Act is designed to protect the general public, not to limit the activities of informed professional investors, such as banks, insurance companies and pension or profit-sharing trusts. Transactions with institutions are exempt.   (Page 61)

25.   **D.**   Neither exempt securities nor exempt transactions are exempt from the antifraud provisions.   (Page 55)

26.   **C.**   The Uniform Securities Act prohibits soliciting orders for unregistered nonexempt securities.   (Page 68)

27.   **C.**   Effecting transactions without specific authority to do so is prohibited.   (Page 67)

28.   **B.**   Making unsuitable recommendations to customers is prohibited.   (Page 67)

29.   **C.**   Repeating rumors is both misleading and prohibited under the Uniform Securities Act.   (Page 68)

30.   **C.**   Disseminating and acting on inside information is prohibited.   (Page 68)

31.   **C.**   If an investment adviser or broker-dealer has custody of customer assets, the state administrator may set a minimum capital or surety bond requirement of $35,000. A broker-dealer in compliance with federal net capital rules is exempt from the state's requirements.   (Page 26)

32.   **D.**   Each of the answers listed is an example of an unlawful activity by an investment adviser.   (Page 67)

33.   **D.**   Securities that do not require registration under the Uniform Securities Act are exempt securities. Although the securities are exempt, the agent who makes the solicitation and his broker-dealer must be registered.   (Page 69)

34.   **D.**   Excessive trading activity in an account is called *churning* and is a prohibited practice.   (Page 67)

35. **A.** Material facts are facts essential for making an investment decision. To omit them is fraudulent or deceitful. (Page 68)

36. **A.** Those persons who act in an advisory capacity in states that do not require registration must register with the SEC. (Page 23)

37. **D.** The Uniform Securities Act requires an agent to forward any written complaints received to his employer. (Page 69)

38. **B.** Clerical and ministerial personnel are not included in the definition of investment adviser representatives (supervised persons). Any other person associated with an investment adviser, including an officer of the firm, is generally considered to be an investment adviser representative. (Page 21)

39. **B.** Trading in a customer's account must not be excessive in terms of size or frequency with respect to the customer's investment objectives and financial ability. Whether the adviser acted as principal or agent, or received compensation, is not a consideration. The customer's approval of the transactions does not release the adviser from abiding by suitability requirements. (Page 67)

40. **B.** Disseminating phony or misleading quotes is a prohibited practice. (Page 69)

41. **C.** Under the NSMIA (National Securities Markets Improvement Act), state administrators are no longer able to exercise full jurisdiction over federally registered advisers. However, administrators must enforce all antifraud regulations for investment advisers practicing within their states. (Page 42)

42. **B.** Registration of a security with the SEC or the state implies neither approval nor disapproval. (Page 67)

43. **D.** If it seems illegal, it probably is a violation. (Page 69)

44. **A.** If an investment adviser demonstrates contempt (contumacy) for an administrator's order or subpoena, a court may be asked to enforce it. The adviser's registration or ability to conduct business may not be affected. (Page 9)

45. **C.** A violation of any state or federal securities or commodities law is grounds for denial, suspension, revocation or cancellation of registration. Convictions are grounds for administrator action if they occurred within the past 10 years. Lack of experience is not sufficient cause for revoking or denying registration. (Page 27)

46. **C.** An administrator may suspend or revoke any registration if he finds that the order is in the public interest *and* he finds guilt of any of the listed offenses. (Page 14)

47. **A.** An administrator may not deny, suspend or revoke registration solely on the basis of lack of experience. (Page 15)

48. **B.** The rescission right of the buyer is to recover the purchase price and interest. If the seller discovers the illegal sale, the seller may offer to repurchase the security. The buyer has 30 days to accept after receiving the rescission letter offering to refund the money and interest; otherwise, the sale stands. (Page 10)

49. **A.** The Uniform Securities Act gives the state administrator jurisdiction (the scope of the act) over transactions originated in, directed to or accepted in the administrator's state. An administrator may suspend any registration if two things are true: (1) it is in the public interest and (2) one of the specific offenses listed has been committed. An administrator must turn over to the court system any cases which suggest criminal penalties. (Page 59)

50. **D.** The administrator in any state to or from which an offer is made has jurisdiction over the offer. (Page 8)

7

Uniform Securities Act Exam Two

1. According to the Uniform Securities Act, a person would be required to register as a broker-dealer in a state under which of the following circumstances?

   I. The person has no place of business in the state, but has directed offers to clients with more than 30 days' temporary residency.
   II. The person has no place of business in the state and deals exclusively with broker-dealers in that state.
   III. The person has no place of business in the state and effects transactions exclusively with issuers of securities in that state.
   IV. The person has a place of business in the state.

   A. I, II and IV only
   B. I and IV only
   C. II and III only
   D. I, II, III and IV

2. Under the Uniform Securities Act, a person representing an issuer of which of the following securities would NOT have to be registered as an agent?

   I. Banker's acceptance
   II. Municipal bond
   III. U.S. bank issue
   IV. Investment contract issued in connection with an employee's stock purchase, savings, pension, profit-sharing or similar benefit plan

   A. I and II only
   B. I, III and IV only
   C. III and IV only
   D. I, II, III and IV

3. Under the Uniform Securities Act, an individual would NOT be considered an agent if he engages in which of the following types of transactions?

   I. Between an issuer and an insurance company
   II. Between an issuer and unsophisticated investors
   III. Between an issuer and the underwriters
   IV. Between an issuer and savings institutions or trust companies

   A. I, III and IV only
   B. II and III only
   C. II and IV only
   D. I, II, III and IV

117

4. An issuer employs its officers and directors to sell newly issued shares of the company. The officers and directors are compensated for the sales. According to the Uniform Securities Act, the officers and directors would have to be registered as agents of the

   A. issuer
   B. broker-dealer
   C. broker-dealer and issuer
   D. state administrator

5. A nonissuer corporation has its employees sell nonexempt securities. The corporation receives a commission on the sale of the securities, and some of the commission is then paid to the employees. According to the Uniform Securities Act, the corporation is a

   A. broker-dealer that must be registered
   B. corporation selling only to sophisticated investors
   C. broker-dealer engaging in exempt transactions
   D. corporation selling to an employee pension fund

6. Under the National Securities Markets Improvement Act, a person with $25,000,000 or more in assets under management must register with the

   A. NASD
   B. NASAA
   C. SEC
   D. NYSE

7. As defined by the Uniform Securities Act, an example of an investment adviser is a

   A. lawyer
   B. publisher of a magazine
   C. person who is paid a fee for advising customers on securities
   D. person who is paid a commission for advising customers on securities

8. An issuer uses its directors to sell stock to employees, for which the directors receive commissions. According to the Uniform Securities Act, which of the following describe the directors?

   I. Agents of the issuer
   II. Agents of a broker-dealer
   III. Need not be licensed
   IV. Must be licensed

   A. I and III
   B. I and IV
   C. II and III
   D. II and IV

9. A corporate officer of an issuer sells securities of that corporation to a bank for a commission. What is his status under the Uniform Securities Act?

   A. He is a broker-dealer.
   B. He is an agent of a broker-dealer.
   C. He must be licensed as an agent.
   D. He need not be licensed as an agent.

10. Under the Uniform Securities Act, which of the following statements about a sale, an offer or an offer and sale is true?

   I. Any security given or delivered with or as a bonus for any purchase of securities is considered to have been offered and sold for value.
   II. A gift of assessable stock is considered to involve an offer and sale.
   III. Every sale or offer of a warrant or stock right to purchase or subscribe to another security is considered to include an offer of the other security.
   IV. Every bona fide pledge is considered an offer and sale.

   A. I, II and III only
   B. I and III only
   C. II and IV only
   D. I, II, III and IV

11. According to the Uniform Securities Act, an offer or a sale does NOT exist if it is a(n)

    I. act as a result of a class vote by stockholders regarding a merger or consolidation
    II. bona fide pledge or loan
    III. act incident to a judicially approved reorganization in which a security is issued in exchange for one or more outstanding shares
    IV. act as a result of a judicially approved reorganization in which one security is issued in exchange for an outstanding security

    A. I and II only
    B. I, II and III only
    C. IV only
    D. I, II, III and IV

12. An interest in which of the following can be defined as a security under the Uniform Securities Act?

    I. Merchandising marketing scheme
    II. Multilevel distributorship arrangement
    III. Oil and gas drilling program

    A. I only
    B. II and III only
    C. III only
    D. I, II and III

13. According to the Uniform Securities Act, the administrator has the power to require the agent licensee to

    A. have minimum net capital, post a surety bond and pass an exam
    B. post a surety bond and pass an exam
    C. post a surety bond, pay filing fees and pass an exam
    D. have minimum net capital, pay filing fees, pass an exam and post a surety bond

14. According to the Uniform Securities Act, after an agent passes the Series 63 exam and an NASD/NYSE licensing exam, when can she begin to sell?

    I. Immediately
    II. When she is affiliated with a broker-dealer
    III. When she has been granted a registration from the state administrator
    IV. When she gets permission from the principal in the office

    A. I
    B. I and IV
    C. II and III
    D. II and IV

15. An agent representing a broker-dealer in Utah wishes to do business in California exclusively in the trading of certain exempt securities. Under the Uniform Securities Act, the agent would

    A. not have to register in California
    B. have to register in California
    C. not have to register if the broker-dealer is registered in California
    D. be allowed to do business because the securities are exempt

16. According to the Uniform Securities Act, under what circumstances is an employee of a licensed broker-dealer firm allowed to sell exempt securities as an unregistered agent?

    A. The securities are exempt.
    B. The transaction is exempt.
    C. The employee is not paid any commission or salary.
    D. Under no circumstances

17. If it is in the public interest to do so, the Uniform Securities Act provides that the state administrator may deny the registration of a person for all of the following reasons EXCEPT

   A. the applicant is not qualified owing to lack of experience
   B. a willful violation of the act has taken place
   C. the applicant is financially insolvent
   D. the applicant is enjoined temporarily from engaging in the securities business

18. If a person is exempt from state registration but is a federally registered investment adviser, what must be done in order to practice within a particular state?

   I. Pay state filing fees
   II. Pass an oral or written examination
   III. Give notice to the state
   IV. Become licensed as a broker-dealer

   A. I and II
   B. I and III
   C. II and III
   D. II and IV

19. Under the Uniform Securities Act, an agent's license is effective for what period of time?

   A. Until December 31st
   B. Eighteen months, of which the first six months is a probationary period
   C. Twenty years
   D. Term of the agent's employment, unless withdrawn or revoked

20. Under the Uniform Securities Act, the administrator may require the filing of which of the following documents?

   I. Prospectus
   II. Pamphlet
   III. Circular
   IV. Advertisement

   A. I, III and IV only
   B. I and IV only
   C. II and III only
   D. I, II, III and IV

21. All of the following are part of the Uniform Securities Act's registration by filing procedure EXCEPT that

   A. companies must have attained a specific level of earnings for the prior three-year period
   B. a copy of the offering circular or prospectus must be filed
   C. if not denied, registration becomes effective after 30 days
   D. a statement must list the name(s) of the underwriter(s) and describe the terms of the offering

22. Under the Uniform Securities Act, an initial public offering registered simultaneously with the state and the SEC will MOST likely be registered by

   A. coordination
   B. qualification
   C. filing
   D. representation

23. Under the Uniform Securities Act, no specific response is required from the state administrator before which of the following types of securities registration becomes effective?

   I. Coordination
  II. Qualification
 III. Filing
 IV. Consanguination

A. I and II only
B. I and III only
C. II, III and IV only
D. I, II, III and IV

24. According to the Uniform Securities Act, the administrator may require an issuer that has an effective registration statement to file reports NOT more than

A. quarterly
B. semiannually
C. annually
D. biennially

25. All of the following statements are true regarding the selling of private placements under the Uniform Securities Act EXCEPT that

A. they cannot be offered to more than 10 persons in 12 consecutive months
B. they cannot be offered to more than 35 persons in 12 consecutive months
C. the seller must reasonably believe that all buyers are purchasing for investment purposes only
D. no commission or other remuneration may be paid for soliciting noninstitutional buyers

26. Registration statements for securities under the Uniform Securities Act are effective for

A. a period of time determined by the administrator for each issue
B. one year from the effective date
C. one year from the date of issue
D. one year from the previous January 1st

27. According to the Uniform Securities Act, which of the following statements are true regarding the registration of securities by coordination?

   I. The cooling-off period for the states is 10 days.
  II. The cooling-off period for the SEC is 20 days.
 III. The registration becomes effective in the state only after the state's cooling-off period.
 IV. The registration becomes effective at the state level in conjunction with the SEC if the administrator has not entered an order to deny it.

A. I, II and IV only
B. I and III only
C. IV only
D. I, II, III and IV

28. All of the following are considered exempt securities under the Uniform Securities Act EXCEPT

   I. U.S. government securities
  II. unsolicited transactions
 III. transactions between issuers and underwriters
 IV. securities of credit unions

A. I, II and IV
B. I and IV
C. II and III
D. IV

29. Investment advisers who manage private investment company portfolios may be compensated by

A. performance-based fees
B. flat fees established by written contract
C. total services fee
D. fees based upon a percentage of net assets under management

30. Which of the following are exempt from state registration as covered securities?

    A. Sales to qualified purchasers
    B. Federally exempt offerings and transactions
    C. Registered investment company securities
    D. All of the above

31. According to the Uniform Securities Act, under which of the following circumstances may an administrator cancel a person's registration?

    A. The person is adjudged to be mentally incompetent.
    B. The administrator determines it would be in the public interest.
    C. The person is the subject of an insider trading lawsuit.
    D. The person has been terminated from employment at an investment adviser firm.

32. According to the Uniform Securities Act, the investment adviser brochure must include the business background of

    A. the investment adviser
    B. employees of the adviser
    C. an affiliated broker-dealer
    D. institutional clients

33. Under the Uniform Securities Act, the state securities administrator may revoke an exemption claimed by which of the following securities issuers?

    A. Nonprofit charitable organization
    B. Canadian province
    C. Common carrier subject to the Interstate Commerce Commission
    D. Federal savings and loan association

34. Under the Uniform Securities Act, which of the following constitutes an offer of a security?

    A. Stock dividend distributed to current shareholders
    B. Agreement between an issuer and an underwriter
    C. Prospectus
    D. Tombstone advertisement

35. A customer is upset with her agent for not servicing her account properly and sends him a complaint letter about his actions. Under the Uniform Securities Act, the agent should

    A. call the customer and apologize, promising to do a better job
    B. tell the customer he is willing to make rescission
    C. do nothing and hope the customer forgets to send the letter
    D. bring the customer complaint to the employer immediately

36. Which of the following would NOT be considered a market manipulation under the Uniform Securities Act?

    A. Three market makers start buying and selling the same security simultaneously in their own accounts.
    B. A specialist buys and sells stock for his own account.
    C. A principal in a broker-dealer allows a rumor to leak out that Microscam is going to acquire Datawaq; after a few days, the broker-dealer sells short for its own account Microscam.
    D. A broker sells a customer's stock at the bid price and makes up the difference with a personal check.

37. In order to get a sale of $10,000 worth of bonds, an agent promises to balance a customer's checkbook each month for as long as the customer lives, even though the agent is in line for a promotion and an office transfer. Under the Uniform Securities Act, this is considered a(n)

    A. acceptable practice
    B. unacceptable practice
    C. practice that is not a violation; however, it is not a wise practice
    D. acceptable practice if it is in accordance with house rules

38. The state administrator revokes the registration of an agent. Under the Uniform Securities Act, the agent may file for a review of the revocation order within how many days of revocation?

    A. 30
    B. 60
    C. 90
    D. 270

39. According to the Uniform Securities Act, market manipulation includes all of the following EXCEPT

    A. buying on one exchange and selling on another
    B. withholding a material fact from a buyer
    C. buying and selling intentionally to show market activity
    D. giving a false quote

40. A customer has a discretionary account with his agent. The objective of the account is current income. The agent purchases a speculative growth stock. Under the Uniform Securities Act, this is considered a(n)

    A. wash sale
    B. unauthorized transaction
    C. acceptable transaction
    D. matching activity

41. Under the Uniform Securities Act, which of the following is responsible for proving that a securities issue is exempt from registration?

    A. Underwriter
    B. Issuer
    C. State administrator
    D. There is no need to prove eligibility for an exemption.

42. According to the Uniform Securities Act, which of the following are fraudulent or deceitful business practices?

    I. Matched order
    II. Phony quote
    III. Material misrepresentation
    IV. Wash sale

    A. I and II only
    B. I, II and III only
    C. III and IV only
    D. I, II, III and IV

43. According to the Uniform Securities Act, which of the following is an example of market manipulation?

    A. Creating the illusion of active trading
    B. Buying on one exchange and selling on another
    C. Guaranteeing performance of a security
    D. Transactions in excess of a customer's financial capability

44. A famous tennis player offers to record a testimonial for an investment adviser for use in a television commercial. Under the Uniform Securities Act, the investment adviser may

    A. use the testimonial as long as the athlete receives no compensation
    B. use the testimonial and may pay the athlete
    C. use the testimonial with the approval of the state administrator
    D. not use the testimonial under any circumstances

45. An agent omits to state facts in which a prudent investor would be interested. Under the Uniform Securities Act, this action is

   A. fraudulent for nonexempt securities only
   B. fraudulent for exempt securities only
   C. fraudulent for both exempt and nonexempt securities
   D. not fraudulent if there was no willful intent to omit the information

46. A customer living in one state receives a phone call from an agent in another state. A transaction between the two occurs in yet another state. According to the Uniform Securities Act, under whose jurisdiction does the transaction fall?

   A. Administrator of the state in which the customer lives
   B. Administrator of the state in which the agent's office is located
   C. Administrator of the state in which the transaction took place
   D. Administrators of all three states involved

47. Under the Uniform Securities Act, an agent who willfully violates state securities law is subject to which of the following?

   I. Civil liabilities
   II. Criminal penalties
   III. Suspension, revocation or barring from registration as an agent by the administrator

   A. I only
   B. I and II only
   C. III only
   D. I, II and III

48. According to the Uniform Securities Act, a person who sells securities in violation of state securities laws is civilly liable for which of the following?

   I. Principal
   II. Interest
   III. Court costs
   IV. Attorney's fees

   A. I, III and IV only
   B. I and IV only
   C. II and III only
   D. I, II, III and IV

49. Under the Uniform Securities Act, an agent's license could be revoked if

   I. he was convicted of a security misdemeanor
   II. he was insolvent
   III. he was judged mentally incompetent

   A. I
   B. I or II
   C. II
   D. III

50. As a result of which of the following would an agent possibly be subject to denial of registration under the Uniform Securities Act?

   I. She has engaged in fraud in selling to an insurance company.
   II. She was convicted of a security misdemeanor eight years ago.
   III. She is insolvent.
   IV. She has failed to pay filing fees.

   A. I only
   B. I, II and III only
   C. II, III and IV only
   D. I, II, III and IV

◆ Answers & Rationale

1. **B.** The term "broker-dealer" does not include a person who has no place of business in the state and who (1) effects transactions exclusively through issuers, other broker-dealers or institutions or (2) directs an offer in the state to an existing customer who has more than 30 days temporary residency within the state where the offer is received. (Page 11)

2. **D.** An individual is not considered an agent when representing the issuer in each of the cases cited. Note that for purposes of the exam, unless otherwise stated, all commercial paper is considered to mature in 270 days or less. (Page 12)

3. **A.** An individual who effects securities transactions for compensation is defined as an agent. A person representing an issuer in an exempt transaction does not fall under the definition, nor does a person who represents an issuer in effecting transactions with existing employees in which no commissions are paid. (Page 12)

4. **A.** The definition of "agent" would include an individual representing the issuer in a transaction for the benefit of the issuer unless the individual does not receive compensation. (Page 12)

5. **A.** A broker-dealer is in the business of effecting transactions in securities for its own account or for the accounts of others. Under the Uniform Securities Act, the broker-dealer must register in the state where business is transacted. (Page 2)

6. **C.** Under current law, persons who have $25 million or more in assets under management must register exclusively with the SEC. These persons are referred to as federally registered investment advisers. (Page 23)

7. **C.** An investment adviser is any person who is in the business of selling investment advice. (Page 20)

8. **B.** Registration as an agent of the issuer is necessary because commissions are paid. (Page 12)

9. **D.** The definition of "agent" does not include an officer of the issuer selling the issuer's securities to a bank (institutional investor). (Page 12)

10. **A.** The term "sale" does not include a bona fide pledge. (Page 3)

11. **D.** The Uniform Securities Act specifically excludes these four choices from the definition of "offer and sale." (Page 4)

12. **D.** Any investment contract entered into for profit where management is performed by someone other than the investors can be considered a security. (Page 4)

13. **C.** The administrator *may* require that, as a condition of registration, the agent post a surety bond, pay filing fees and pass an examination that may be written, oral or both. (Page 13)

14. **C.** Passing an NASD or NYSE licensing exam qualifies an individual to solicit security sales on a federal level. The state administrator must grant registration and the individual must be associated with a broker-dealer before she may engage in securities transactions. (Page 14)

15. **B.** Although the securities are exempted from registration, typically, the agent must register in every state where business is attempted. (Page 12)

16. **D.** It is unlawful for a person to transact business unless that person is registered, even if the securities are exempt. (Page 12)

17. **A.** Registration may be denied if the applicant willfully violates the Uniform Securi-

ties Act, is financially insolvent or has been enjoined from engaging in the securities business. If the person qualifies by virtue of training or knowledge, registration cannot be denied for lack of experience only.   (Page 15)

18. **B.**   While exempt from state registration, federally registered investment advisers must "give notice" (written) and pay state filing fees to practice within the given states.   (Page 23)

19. **A.**   An agent's license is not valid immediately after the agent passes the Uniform Securities Examination; rather, it is issued 30 days after he meets all registration requirements. Once the agent terminates employment with a broker-dealer, his license is no longer valid. Registration must be renewed annually or it will expire on December 31st.   (Page 13)

20. **D.**   The administrator may require the filing of any advertising or sales literature. Prospectuses, pamphlets, circulars and advertisements can fall under the definition of "advertising and sales literature." However, registered investment companies are exempt from state registration and filing requirements.   (Page 58)

21. **C.**   Registration by filing becomes effective concurrently with federal effectiveness.
(Page 57)

22. **A.**   Both registration by filing and registration by coordination become effective when the security is released by the SEC. However, an initial public offering may not be registered by filing; the security will therefore be registered by coordination.   (Page 57)

23. **B.**   Registration by coordination and by filing do not require a specific response from the state administrator.   (Page 57)

24. **A.**   As long as the registration is effective, the administrator may require the person who filed the registration statement to file quarterly reports. The reports update information contained

in the registration statement and disclose the progress of the offering.   (Page 59)

25. **B.**   This question distinguishes the differences in federal and state requirements for private placements. Under state law, a private placement can be offered to no more than 10 non-accredited investors.   (Page 62)

26. **B.**   Securities registration statements are effective for one year from the effective date.
(Page 58)

27. **A.**   The federal 1933 securities act requires that securities offered to the public be registered with the SEC. The registration statement becomes effective on the 20th calendar day following the date the statement is received by the SEC (assuming the SEC does not find any deficiencies or misrepresentations). During the 20-day cooling-off period between the filing date and the effective date, indications of interest from the public for shares may be taken. When the registration becomes effective, shares in the new issue may be reconfirmed and actual orders taken. Note that on the federal level, the registration must be on file with the SEC for 20 days, while on the state level it must be on file with the administration for at least 10 days.   (Page 57)

28. **C.**   You must be able to distinguish between an exempt security and an exempt transaction.   (Page 60)

29. **A.**   Investment company advisers are typically prohibited from accepting performance-based compensation. However, advisers who manage private investment company portfolios can now accept compensation in the form of performance-based fees.   (Page 35)

30. **D.**   Covered securities are exempt from state registration. These securities include listed securities, registered investment company securities (funds), private investment company sales, and offerings and transactions exempt on a federal level.   (Page 59)

31. **A.** Registration may be canceled by the administrator if the registered person has been adjudged mentally incompetent. Merely being the subject of a lawsuit, without being convicted of the crime, is not grounds for cancellation. A person's registration is not in effect any time when the person is no longer associated with an employing firm. However, the registration has not been canceled. (Page 28)

32. **A.** The business background of any person who will be responsible for making investment recommendations must be included in Part II of the Form ADV filed for registration; substantially the same information must be provided in the disclosure brochure. (Page 32)

33. **A.** The state administrator has the authority to deny or revoke the exempt status of a security issued by a religious or charitable organization or by an employee benefit plan; he may also deny or revoke the exempt status of any exempt transaction. (Page 59)

34. **C.** A prospectus is the document that offers a security for sale. A tombstone advertisement is not considered an offer of the security; it is used to solicit indications of interest. An agreement between an issuer and an underwriter is not considered an offer to purchase or sell the security; and the definition of offer and sale specifically excludes stock dividends. (Page 3)

35. **D.** Failure to bring customers' written complaints to the attention of the agent's broker-dealer is prohibited. (Page 69)

36. **B.** The function of the specialist normally is to act as a broker for orders left with him by other members and to act as a dealer in buying and selling for his own account. (Page 68)

37. **B.** An agent may not make promises that probably cannot be kept. (Page 69)

38. **B.** If a person wishes to appeal a final order of the state administrator, a written petition may be filed with the appropriate court within 60 days of the entry of the order. The court may then affirm or set aside the revocation order.

(Page 14)

39. **A.** Buying on one exchange and selling on another is known as "arbitrage." This is an accepted trading practice. (Page 67)

40. **B.** The customer authorized the agent to buy income-producing securities only. Wash sale and matching activity refer to creating the impression of activity in a stock by buying and selling the same stock at the same price without a change in beneficial ownership. These activities may cause others to buy or sell the security.

(Page 67)

41. **B.** The burden of proof for claiming eligibility for an exemption falls to the person claiming the exemption. (Page 60)

42. **D.** Both matched orders and wash sales distort the actual trading activity in a security. Phony quotes and material misrepresentations are untrue statements of fact and are therefore prohibited. (Page 67)

43. **A.** Creating the illusion of trading activity is a manipulation of the market. Arbitrage (choice B) is not market manipulation. Guaranteeing performance of a security is prohibited because they are untrue statements; however, it is not market manipulation. Trades that are too large for a customer also are prohibited because they are not suitable, but they are not considered market manipulation. (Page 68)

44. **D.** Under the Uniform Securities Act, advertising materials are deemed to be misleading if they are in violation of the Investment Advisers Act's advertising requirements. Testimonials are specifically prohibited under both state and federal law. (Page 38)

45. **C.** The omission of a material fact in the sale, purchase or offer of a security is fraudulent. This applies whether the security being offered is exempt or nonexempt. (Page 68)

46. **D.** The Uniform Securities Act gives the state administrator jurisdiction over offers to buy or sell when the offers originate in or are directed to the administrator's state or are accepted in that state.   (Page 8)

47. **D.** Violations of securities laws are subject to criminal penalties, civil liabilities and denial, suspension or revocation of registration.
(Page 15)

48. **D.** The person illegally selling the securities is liable for the purchase price of the securities plus interest from the date of purchase, costs and reasonable attorney's fees.   (Page 10)

49. **B.** A license may be revoked if it is in the public interest and the administrator ascertains that the agent is insolvent or has a criminal record.   (Page 15)

50. **D.** Fraud, conviction of a felony or misdemeanor involving a security and insolvency are grounds for denial.   (Page 15)

8

1. You are a broker having lunch with your grandfather, who is head of Datawaq. He tells you that the government did not approve a large contract, which will hurt Datawaq's profits next year. According to the Uniform Securities Act, you should

    A. tell your best customers to sell their holdings of the corporation
    B. inform your broker-dealer of this promptly
    C. call the "60 Minutes" team
    D. sell Datawaq short so you do not get left out of the trading

2. A financial contract can best be defined as which of the following?

    A. The purchase of a whole life insurance policy
    B. The purchase of exchange-listed stock shares
    C. A negotiated transaction with lawful consideration
    D. The signing of an investment adviser's agreement with an investment company

3. According to the Uniform Securities Act, which of the following are considered securities?

    I. HR-10 or Keogh accounts
    II. Commercial paper
    III. IRAs
    IV. Voting trust certificates

    A. I and II
    B. I, III and IV
    C. II
    D. II and IV

4. Under the Uniform Securities Act, a state administrator may appoint another officer to

    A. serve subpoenas
    B. grant registration exemptions
    C. issue a cease and desist order
    D. set recordkeeping requirements

5. Which of the following is an example of a nonissuer transaction as defined by the Uniform Securities Act?

    A. Private placement
    B. Secondary offering
    C. Primary issue of a corporation
    D. Preemptive offering

6. Violations of the Uniform Securities Act can be punishable by

   A. civil liabilities
   B. criminal penalties
   C. license suspension
   D. all of the above

7. Under the Uniform Securities Act, which of the following is(are) considered a sale(s)?

   I. Gift of an assessable stock
   II. Gift of an ordinary stock
   III. Security given as a bonus for purchasing a bond
   IV. Offer of securities

   A. I
   B. I and II
   C. I and III
   D. II, III and IV

8. If convicted of a willful violation of the Uniform Securities Act, an agent may be subject to a maximum of

   A. imprisonment for five years
   B. a fine of $5,000 and/or imprisonment for three years
   C. a fine of $10,000
   D. disbarment

9. As defined by the Uniform Securities Act, secondary trades are also known as

   A. private placements
   B. issuer transactions
   C. nonissuer transactions
   D. exempt transactions

10. Under the Uniform Securities Act, which of the following can be distributed if an issuing company has applied for registration by qualification, but the security has not yet been cleared for sale?

    I. Tombstone advertising
    II. Red herring
    III. Application with down payment
    IV. Registration statement

    A. I
    B. I, II and IV
    C. II and III
    D. II and IV

11. According to the Uniform Securities Act, all of the following are violations of suitability requirements EXCEPT failing to

    A. identify customer objectives
    B. identify terms and fees on the customer's contract
    C. make reasonable inquiry of the customer's security holdings
    D. determine the customer's ability to take on risk

12. An agent tells a customer that one of the customer's stocks is worth $10 more per share than it is really worth. Under the Uniform Securities Act, this activity is

    A. allowed if the agent explains that the difference is a service charge
    B. allowed if the customer makes a profit from the end result
    C. misrepresentation and a fraudulent act
    D. misrepresentation without written permission from the branch

13. Under the Uniform Securities Act, which of the following activities are market manipulations?

   I. Disseminating false information
   II. Giving market quotes that can be misinterpreted easily
   III. Selling securities in large amounts to help keep prices down
   IV. Entering matched buy and sell orders to attract attention to the security

   A. I and II only
   B. I, III and IV only
   C. II and III only
   D. I, II, III and IV

14. As defined by the Uniform Securities Act, which of the following activities is an example of churning?

   A. Frequent purchases one day and sales of the same stock the next day in order to align with a customer's investment objectives
   B. Bond swaps
   C. Frequent purchases and sales of load mutual fund shares in a single account
   D. Day trading

15. Under the Uniform Securities Act, which of the following are NOT considered securities?

   I. Commodity futures contract
   II. Commodity options contract
   III. Voting trust certificate
   IV. Insurance contract

   A. I and II
   B. I and IV
   C. II, HI and IV
   D. II and IV

16. Of the following, which are violations of the Uniform Securities Act?

   I. Arbitrage
   II. Soliciting investors for unregistered nonexempt securities
   III. Selling bonds of a foreign government to residents of a state other than the one in which the agent of a broker-dealer is registered and is paid a commission
   IV. Selling T bonds without being registered as an agent of a broker-dealer and not receiving a commission

   A. I and IV only
   B. II and III only
   C. II, III and IV only
   D. I, II, III and IV

17. A customer placed an order with an investment adviser to sell 100 shares of ALF in order to have cash for an urgent purchase the next day, and instructed the adviser to limit any losses. The adviser did not have discretionary authority over the account. The adviser waited to sell the shares, hoping to get a better price for the customer. The price of the shares went down, so the adviser sold 50 ALF shares to limit the customer's losses. According to the Uniform Securities Act, this is a

   A. violation because the adviser acted without discretionary authority
   B. permissible activity because the adviser is obligated to get the best price for the customer
   C. violation because the adviser is required to execute sell transactions immediately after the order is placed
   D. permissible activity because the adviser is not permitted to guarantee a price to a customer

18. An investment adviser is a subsidiary of a broker-dealer. The adviser is the subject of a civil lawsuit alleging a fraudulent sale of securities to a customer. Under the Uniform Securities Act, the brokerage firm may be held jointly liable for the violation EXCEPT if the firm

   A. received payment or another benefit from the transaction
   B. has a record of similar violations
   C. could not have reasonably known about the transaction
   D. discussed the purchase with the customer

19. A sole proprietor incorporates and then sells stock in his company. Under the Uniform Securities Act, the company would be considered a(n)

   A. broker-dealer
   B. exempted proprietorship
   C. issuer
   D. agent

20. A customer is retired, in a low tax bracket and living on a fixed income. An agent recommends and sells to the customer a portfolio of municipal bonds. Under the Uniform Securities Act, what can the administrator do about this?

   A. Force the agent to offer rescission
   B. Revoke the agent's license for selling an unsuitable investment
   C. Suspend the agent's license until the bonds mature
   D. Nothing, because the customer agreed to the purchase

21. Karen Kodiak works for a broker-dealer that is registered in all 50 states. Karen is a registered representative in Nebraska. Klaus Bruin is a customer living and registered to vote in Florida. Klaus calls Karen at her office in Nebraska and offers to purchase securities. Under the Uniform Securities Act, Karen should

   A. accept the order because her broker-dealer is registered in all 50 states
   B. accept the order because she received it in Nebraska
   C. reject the order because she is not registered in Florida
   D. reject the order because it was not a wire order

22. An agent executes a trade in a customer's individual account for the customer. Three days later, when the security is trading three points higher, the customer's husband calls and tells the agent to liquidate the account because the customer has lost her job. Under the Uniform Securities Act, the agent can

   A. write the customer a personal check for the original amount and keep the appreciation as commission
   B. cancel the trade, but retain the commission
   C. cancel the trade
   D. do nothing

23. A millionaire wants to invest in an income portfolio. An agent, acting with discretionary power, invests the customer's money in a portfolio of stock stressing appreciation and little, if any, income. Under the Uniform Securities Act, this activity is

   A. ethical because the customer will make more money
   B. illegal because the customer must make the investment decision
   C. unsuitable
   D. all of the above

24. An agent hears a rumor concerning an investment and uses the information to influence a customer who has hesitated to make the purchase. Under the Uniform Securities Act, which of the following statements is true?

    A. Because the agent made it clear that it was a rumor, this is not a violation.
    B. Because the customer knew it was a rumor and therefore could not be reliable, this is not a violation.
    C. Because rumors are not considered to be inside information, this is not a violation.
    D. Under no circumstances would this be allowed.

25. Under the Uniform Securities Act, an agent may NOT make which of the following statements to a customer?

    A. "This security is registered with the state."
    B. "This security is cleared by the administrator."
    C. "This security is approved for sale by the administrator."
    D. "This security is exempt from registration."

26. An agent receives inside information concerning the possibility of an impending merger. Under the Uniform Securities Act, the agent may divulge the information to

    A. his best customers three days prior to a public announcement
    B. anyone three days prior to a public announcement
    C. the broker-dealer three days after public notice
    D. anyone after public notice

27. When a broker-dealer's registration under the Uniform Securities Act is revoked, which of the following occur(s)?

    I. The registrations of agents of that firm are no longer in effect.
    II. The registrations of agents of that firm are still in effect.
    III. The agent's registration is held in escrow until the broker-dealer gets out of jail.
    IV. One of the agents must be appointed the new broker-dealer.

    A. I
    B. I and III
    C. II
    D. II and IV

28. Which of the following stocks qualifies for the blue chip exemption provided by the Uniform Securities Act?

    A. Stock of a corporation with $10 million in net worth
    B. Stock of a corporation that is listed on the NYSE
    C. Stock of a bank holding company
    D. Stock of a municipal issuer

29. Under the Uniform Securities Act, a registered agent could offer securities for purchase during the underwriting period and before the effective date of registration in which of the following circumstances?

    I. Never
    II. With the use of a red herring
    III. If the securities are not exempt
    IV. Only if a bona fide registration statement has been properly filed with the state administrator and the SEC

    A. I
    B. II
    C. II, III and IV
    D. II and IV

30. According to the Uniform Securities Act, which of the following are considered securities?

   I. Condominium project with a rental pool agreement
   II. U.S. Treasury bill
   III. Limited partnership in an oil and gas exploration program
   IV. Contract in soybean futures

   A. I and II only
   B. I, II and III only
   C. III only
   D. I, II, III and IV

31. If an agent receives a commission from both a broker-dealer and an issuer, under the Uniform Securities Act she is considered an agent of

   A. the issuer
   B. the broker-dealer
   C. both the issuer and the broker-dealer
   D. neither the issuer nor the broker-dealer

32. A president of a bank sells shares of the bank and receives a commission. Under the Uniform Securities Act, he is

   A. a broker-dealer for the bank
   B. an agent of the issuer
   C. an investment adviser
   D. none of the above

33. Which of the following are defined as "supervised persons"?

   I. Partner of an investment advisory firm
   II. Officer of an investment advisory firm
   III. Director of an investment advisory firm
   IV. Investment adviser representative

   A. I and IV only
   B. II, III and IV only
   C. I, II and III only
   D. I, II, III and IV

34. Under the Uniform Securities Act, which of the following is(are) NOT considered a security(ies)?

   I. Secondary sale of a bank mortgage as a pass-through certificate
   II. Limited partnership unit in a cattle-breeding program
   III. Purchase of a condominium as a vacation home
   IV. Franchise agreement where a profit has been promised in the agreement

   A. I and II
   B. I, II and III
   C. I, II and IV
   D. III

35. Which of the following would fall under the Uniform Securities Act's definition of "person"?

   I. Government subdivision
   II. Closely held corporation
   III. Individual
   IV. Parent and child in a custodial account

   A. I only
   B. I and II only
   C. III and IV only
   D. I, II, III and IV

36. According to the Uniform Securities Act, all of the following can provide manual exemptions for a nonissuer distributor of an outstanding security EXCEPT

   A. *Moody's Public Utility Manual*
   B. *Best's Life Insurance Manual*
   C. the Dow Jones Industrial Average
   D. *Fitch's Manual*

37. All of the following practices are prohibited by the Uniform Securities Act EXCEPT

   I. borrowing money from a customer without the customer's written permission
   II. failing to determine adequately the suitability of an investment for a customer
   III. offering rescission
   IV. telling a customer that past history of an investment is not indicative of future results

   A. I and II
   B. I, II and IV
   C. II, III and IV
   D. III and IV

38. An investment adviser may not have custody of a customer's funds and securities under the Uniform Securities Act if

   A. there is a rule barring such custody
   B. the adviser fails to tell the customer that he has custody
   C. the adviser is not a registered broker-dealer
   D. the customer is not a registered adviser recipient

39. According to the Uniform Securities Act, a person representing an issuer of which of the following securities would have to be registered as an agent?

   I. Commercial paper
   II. Municipal bonds
   III. Securities of a U.S. bank
   IV. Investment contracts issued in connection with an employee stock purchase, savings, pension, profit-sharing or similar benefit plan

   A. I and II
   B. I, III and IV
   C. II and IV
   D. None of the above

40. An issuer employs its officers and directors to sell newly issued shares of the company and compensates them for the sales. To comply with the Uniform Securities Act, the officers and directors would have to be registered as agents of

   A. the issuer
   B. the broker-dealer
   C. the broker-dealer and the issuer
   D. neither the broker-dealer nor the issuer because the transactions are exempt

41. The purpose of a private investment company is to

   A. raise capital for business ventures
   B. raise capital for publicly traded corporations
   C. attract capital that will be managed by fee-based advisers
   D. allow advisers to have another product to offer clients

42. An issuer uses its directors to sell stock to employees, for which the directors receive commissions. Under the Uniform Securities Act, the directors

   I. are agents of the issuer
   II. are agents of a broker-dealer
   III. need not be licensed
   IV. must be licensed

   A. I and III
   B. I and IV
   C. II and III
   D. II and IV

43. According to the Uniform Securities Act, which of the following are considered sales, offers or offers and sales?

   I. Any security given or delivered with or as a bonus for any purchase of securities
   II. Any gift of assessable stock
   III. Every sale or offer of a warrant or stock right to purchase or subscribe to another security
   IV. Bona fide pledge

   A. I, II and III only
   B. I and III only
   C. II and IV only
   D. I, II, III and IV

44. Advisers of private investment companies may be compensated by which of the following fee structures?

   A. Commission
   B. Hourly rate
   C. Performance fee
   D. Trading stamps

45. According to the Uniform Securities Act, after an agent passes the Series 63 exam and a Series 6, 7 or 22 exam, when can she begin to sell?

   I. Immediately
   II. When she is affiliated with a broker-dealer
   III. When she has been granted a registration from the state administrator
   IV. When she gets permission from the principal in the office

   A. I
   B. I and IV
   C. II and III
   D. II and IV

46. Under the Uniform Securities Act, an employee of a licensed broker-dealer firm is allowed to sell exempt securities as an unregistered agent in which of the following cases?

   A. The securities are exempt.
   B. The transactions are exempt.
   C. The employee is not paid any commission or salary.
   D. Under no circumstances

47. Which of the following requirements are common to the registration of agents, state-registered investment advisers and broker-dealers under the Uniform Securities Act?

   I. The person must file, along with the application, a consent to service.
   II. The person's registration is two years in length.
   III. The person may be required to pass a written exam.
   IV. The person may be required to post a surety bond.

   A. I and III only
   B. I, III and IV only
   C. II and IV only
   D. I, II, III and IV

48. Qualified purchasers include all of the following EXCEPT

   A. individual with $5 million in investments
   B. family-owned business with $5 million in investments
   C. business with $5 million in investments
   D. trust sponsored by qualified purchasers

49. A registered broker-dealer gives investment advice as part of its business. One of its registered representatives gives investment advice outside the scope of his employment at the firm. Under SEC Release IA-1092, which of the following statements is(are) true?

    I. The broker-dealer must register as an investment adviser.
    II. The rep must register as an investment adviser.
    III. The rep need not register as an investment adviser.
    IV. The broker-dealer need not register as an investment adviser.

    A. I and II
    B. I and III
    C. II and IV
    D. III

50. Broker-dealers are exempt from state registration under which of the following circumstances?

    A. The broker-dealer is federally registered.
    B. The broker-dealer is also an investment adviser.
    C. The broker-dealer's client has less than 30 days' temporary residency within the state.
    D. The broker-dealer's client has less than 60 days' temporary residency within the state.

◆ Answers & Rationale

1. **B.** If you receive inside information, you should inform your supervisor immediately so that he may take the appropriate steps to avoid any transaction that may be construed to violate the Uniform Securities Act.   (Page 68)

2. **C.** A financial contract is a binding agreement entered into to meet the objectives of both parties.   (Page 34)

3. **D.** Individual retirement accounts and Keogh plans are types of customer accounts, not types of securities.   (Page 4)

4. **A.** An official designated by the administrator may carry out the functions of the administrator with regard to investigating violations of the USA. The other activities described are responsibilities of the administrator and may not be delegated.   (Page 9)

5. **C.** "Nonissuer transaction" is defined as any transaction that does not benefit the issuer. Choices I, III and IV would provide the issuer with capital and, therefore, a benefit. In a secondary offering, the seller, not the issuer, receives the benefit.   (Page 61)

6. **D.** Violations of securities law will come under the scrutiny of both state and federal jurisdictions, the SEC and the NASD.   (Page 10)

7. **C.** A "sale" is defined as a contract or transaction for value. Because an assessable stock may have value, the gift is considered a sale. A warrant is both an offer and a sale. Gifts of stock are not sales, and choice IV is an offer, not a sale.   (Page 3)

8. **B.** Under the act, the maximum penalty is a fine of $5,000 and/or three years in jail. These penalties may be in addition to other penalties.   (Page 10)

9. **C.** Secondary transactions are transactions that do not benefit the issuer. Issuer transactions and private placements are primary offerings.   (Page 61)

10. **B.** Prior to clearance, a red herring may be distributed to estimate or gauge customer interest. Additionally, the registration statement may be distributed (although normally it is not). A tombstone advertisement is also allowed.   (Page 46)

11. **B.** Failure to identify objectives or to obtain corresponding financial information is considered contrary to the know-your-customer rule.   (Page 67)

12. **C.** In this situation, aside from misrepresenting the value of the stock, the agent has committed a fraudulent act. Fraudulent acts are not part of selling.   (Page 69)

13. **D.** Any action to influence the price of a security is considered market manipulation. Stating falsehoods, misrepresenting prices, matching and placing orders to influence prices are all examples of manipulation.   (Page 68)

14. **C.** "Churning" is defined as excessive activity in a customer's account for the sole purpose of generating commissions. As long as the trading is sanctioned by the customer, churning does not occur. Because mutual funds carry a front-end load and are considered long-term investment vehicles, frequent trades constitute churning.   (Page 67)

15. **B.** Commodity futures contracts are not securities, but options are. The other items that are not securities are life insurance contracts, endowment contracts, fixed annuities and IRA and Keogh plans. A voting trust certificate is issued in place of a stock certificate to stockholders of a corporation that is temporarily managed by a voting trust.   (Page 4)

16. **B.** Arbitrage is not a violation. An individual selling exempt securities such as government securities, both foreign and domestic, is not

considered an agent and does not have to register as such as long as no commission is collected. If a commission is collected, that individual would have to be registered. (Page 68)

17. **A.** An investment adviser may determine the price and timing of a transaction without discretionary authority. In this situation, the adviser acted without authority when he changed the amount of the security sold. (Page 67)

18. **C.** In general, supervisors and employers may be held jointly liable for violations committed by any person under their direct or indirect control. This includes a firm that is in a position to manage or influence the activities of a subsidiary firm. The controlling firm may be released from liability if it establishes that it did not know of the violation and could not reasonably have known of it. (Page 10)

19. **C.** Under the USA, any person who issues or proposes to issue any security is an issuer. The company is considered an issuer. (Page 3)

20. **B.** The keys here are "low tax bracket" and "fixed income." A portfolio of municipal bonds is an unsuitable investment. The customer would be better off to buy bonds that pay a higher rate of return. Because the agent failed to make a suitable recommendation, the administrator could revoke the agent's license. (Page 67)

21. **C.** Typically, both the broker-dealer and the agent must be registered in each state in which they plan to do business. In order for the agent to accept the order, either she would have to be registered in Florida or the customer would have to be present in her office in Nebraska. (Page 11)

22. **D.** The key here is "individual account." The only individual who can place an order is the person who has the account. The customer's husband can tell the agent to sell until he is blue in the face, but the agent cannot do so. (Page 67)

23. **C.** This investment is unsuitable because the investor wants income only. The agent has

discretionary power over the account; therefore, the transaction is not illegal. (Page 34)

24. **D.** The use of information that has no basis in fact is strictly prohibited. The use of rumors is misrepresentation and a violation of the Uniform Securities Act. (Page 68)

25. **C.** The state administrator does not *approve anything*. The other statements are statements of fact and are permitted. (Page 68)

26. **D.** After the information has become public, it is no longer considered inside information and may be disseminated. (Page 68)

27. **A.** An agent's license is effective only as long as that agent is associated with a registered broker-dealer. (Page 14)

28. **B.** Companies whose securities are listed on a national exchange, such as the NYSE or AMEX, qualify for the blue chip exemption. Companies that are listed must provide periodic reports concerning their firms, and the reports must be available to prospective investors. (Page 61)

29. **A.** During the cooling-off period, indications of interest may be solicited with the use of a red herring. No offers or sales can be made prior to the registration's effective date. (Page 69)

30. **B.** Except for those items specifically exempted from the definition of "security" (such as life insurance), almost anything can be a security. However, certain items, such as futures contracts, are not securities; therefore, choice IV is incorrect. (Page 4)

31. **C.** For securities purposes, it is necessary only that the individual represent the broker-dealer or the issuer. Receiving a commission from the sale of securities from either the broker-dealer or the issuer satisfies the basic definition of "agent." (Page 12)

32. **D.** Securities of a bank are exempt securities, and a person who transacts business only in exempt securities is, by definition, not an agent or a broker-dealer. (Page 12)

33. **D.** A "supervised person" is an individual who provides investment advice and services on the investment adviser's behalf. This individual is subject to the supervision and control of the investment adviser. (Page 21)

34. **D.** A vacation home is not a security; however, if the condominium had been purchased to rent out, it may be a security. (Page 4)

35. **D.** All of these are "persons" in law. The legal definition of "person" does not include a minor, a deceased individual or a mentally incompetent individual. (Page 20)

36. **C.** *Moody's Public Utility Manual, Fitch's Manual* and *Best's Life Insurance Manual* are all recognized manuals that provide the information necessary for an investor to make an informed investment choice, thus qualifying for the manual exemption. Dow Jones is a market average, not a manual. (Page 61)

37. **D.** The exceptions are offering rescission and explaining that performance is not necessarily guaranteed. (Page 68)

38. **A.** If there is a rule barring custody, under no circumstances may the adviser have custody of customer funds or securities. (Page 34)

39. **D.** An individual is not considered an agent when representing the issuer in each of the cases cited. Note that, for purposes of the exam and unless otherwise stated, all commercial paper is considered to mature in 270 days or less. (Page 12)

40. **A.** The definition of "agent" would include an individual representing the issuer in a transaction for the benefit of the issuer unless the individual does not receive compensation. (Page 12)

41. **A.** Private investment companies represent an unregistered form of investment companies. Their purpose is to raise capital for business ventures. (Page 22)

42. **B.** Registration as an agent of the issuer is necessary because commissions are paid. (Page 12)

43. **A.** The term "sale" does not include a bona fide pledge or loan. (Page 4)

44. **C.** Advisers of private investment companies may be compensated on a performance-fee basis. (Page 35)

45. **C.** Passing the Series 6 (mutual funds and variable annuities), Series 7 (general securities) or Series 22 (direct participation programs) qualifies an individual to solicit security sales on a federal level. The state administrator must grant registration and the individual must be associated with a broker-dealer before the individual may engage in securities transactions. (Page 13)

46. **D.** It is unlawful for a person to transact business unless that person is registered, even if the securities are exempt. (Page 12)

47. **B.** Broker-dealers, agents and state-registered investment advisers must file consent to service of process forms with initial applications for registration. The consent to service gives the administrator rights over the applicants. Each applicant may be required to pass an exam and post a surety bond. Federally registered investment advisers must give notice and pay a filing fee in any state in which they conduct business. (Page 13)

48. **C.** Qualified purchasers are eligible to invest in private investment companies. These persons fall into four categories: (1) individuals with $5 million in investments, (2) trusts sponsored by qualified purchasers, (3) family businesses with $5 million or more invested and (4) business with no less than $25 million invested. (Page 22)

Dearborn
Publishing Group, Inc.

• Dearborn Financial Institute, Inc.®
• Dearborn Financial Publishing, Inc.®
• Dearborn • R&R Newkirk™

• Dearborn Trade™
• Real Estate Education Company®
• Upstart Publishing Company, Inc.™

DIRECT INQUIRIES TO: DRIVE
CHICAGO, IL. 60606
1-800-824-8742

PAGE: 1

ORDER NUMBER: A-719060
ORDER DATE: 4/14/98
CUSTOMER NUMBER: 0-CON019-60

RETURN TO: DEARBORN CH DISTRIBUTION
5 S. 250 FRONTENAC RD.
NAPERVILLE, IL. 60563

BILL TO:
CONSUMER INS SERVICES OF AMERI
LAUREN GRAY
100 CUMMINGS CENTER/SUITE 206C

BEVERLY   MA 01915
CUSTOMER PO: T KLEEKAMP

SHIP TO:
THOMAS KLEEKAMP
512 EMBNERS DRIVE

MARIETTA   GA 30067

DEPT: IL

BATCH: TUE006
SHIP VIA: UNITED PARCEL SERVICE

ITEM NO.	QTY.ORDERED	DESCRIPTION	O.F.	CHK.	PACK	CTNS.
		****** CLASSROOM MATERIALS ******				
		** PLEASE DISTRIBUTE IMMEDIATELY **				
07793128447	1	SER 63 CLASS				
		T KLEEKAMP /25986437 7				
		CLASS DATE 06-14-98 CLASS # 3000638060 16				
		LOCATION: ATLANTA GA				
	1	END OF ORDER **************************				

9-5-98

49. **C.** Broker-dealers and registered reps who give advice as part of their normal business are not required to register as investment advisers. However, if a registered rep provides investment advice outside the scope of employment at the broker-dealer, the rep must be registered. Thus, both choice II and choice IV are true statements.

(Page 28)

50. **C.** Broker-dealers with no office in the state and clients with less than 30 days' temporary residency are exempt from state registration.

(Page 11)

9   Uniform Securities Act Exam Four

1. Under the Uniform Securities Act, an investment adviser may select which of the following to execute customer transactions?

   I. Full-service broker-dealer
   II. Discount broker-dealer
   III. Broker-dealer associated with the investment adviser
   IV. Another investment adviser

   A. I only
   B. II only
   C. II and III only
   D. I, II, III and IV

2. Under the Uniform Securities Act, which of the following persons is included in the definition of "investment adviser"?

   A. Antiques dealer who receives a fee for advising customers as to the value of antiques and rare coins
   B. Registered representative of a broker-dealer who receives a flat fee for analyzing a customer's investment objectives and recommending a portfolio of securities
   C. Publisher that receives a yearly subscription fee for a newsletter that provides nonspecific investment advice
   D. Bank that offers investment counseling to its high net worth customers

3. An agent discovers that he has sold to a customer an unregistered nonexempt security that he thought was exempt. The agent offers to buy it back. Under the Uniform Securities Act, which of the following statements is(are) true?

   I. The customer may accept the offer, but still may sue.
   II. This is legal and is called *rescission*.
   III. The offer also must include interest.
   IV. This cannot be done under any circumstances.

   A. I
   B. II
   C. II and III
   D. IV

4. A customer living in one state receives a phone call from an agent in another state. A transaction between the two occurs in yet another state. Under the Uniform Securities Act, under whose jurisdiction does the transaction fall?

   A. Administrator of the state in which the customer lives
   B. Administrator of the state in which the agent is registered
   C. Administrator of the state in which the transaction took place
   D. Administrators of all three states involved

5. According to the Uniform Securities Act, the sale of a security to an insurance company is

    A. an exempt security
    B. an exempt transaction
    C. always a private placement
    D. illegal

6. Under the NSMIA, issuers are required to pay

    A. federal filing fees
    B. state filing fees
    C. both state and federal filing fees
    D. none of the above

7. All of the following are prohibited practices under the Uniform Securities Act EXCEPT

    I.   borrowing money or securities from a customer's account without express written permission
    II. failing to identify a customer's financial objectives
    III. selling rights
    IV. guaranteeing a customer's account against losses

    A. I and II
    B. I, II and III
    C. I, II and IV
    D. III

8. According to the Uniform Securities Act, which of the following statements regarding state registration of securities is true?

    A. Registration by filing is effective when so ordered by the administrator.
    B. Registration by coordination is effective concurrently with federal registration.
    C. Registration by qualification is effective after 30 days.
    D. Registration by coordination is effective when so ordered by the administrator.

9. According to the Uniform Securities Act, under which of the following circumstances is an agent allowed to tell a customer that, when dividends are reinvested in a mutual fund, the customer always will be able to sell at a profit?

    A. The agent does not use the word "guaranteed."
    B. The agent further explains that dividends reinvested are not taxable income.
    C. The fund is a no-load fund.
    D. This is not permitted under any circumstances.

10. What information may be contained in the advertising prospectus of a management investment company?

    A. Management fees
    B. Sales charges
    C. Investment risks
    D. Performance figures

11. According to the Uniform Securities Act, when an agent leaves one broker-dealer to join another broker-dealer, the agent's license must be changed over

    A. immediately
    B. within 45 days
    C. at the agent's next license renewal date
    D. The agent's license cannot be changed.

12. Which of the following would be defined as a qualified purchaser?

    A. Stuart and Carol, who invest jointly and own $5.5 million in securities
    B. Stuart, who owns $1 million in securities
    C. Adam, who owns a $100,000 house and $1 million in securities
    D. Allison, who is the beneficiary of a $1 million variable life insurance policy and owns $4.9 million in securities

13. States may require a surety bond as a prerequisite to registration under the Uniform Securities Act for which of the following persons?

    I. Broker-dealer
    II. Agent
    III. State-registered investment adviser

    A. I only
    B. I and II only
    C. II and III only
    D. I, II and III

14. The SEC's role now includes

    A. improvement and oversight of market efficiency
    B. competition in the securities industry
    C. capital formation
    D. all of the above

15. According to the Uniform Securities Act, the investment adviser (with the exception of a private investment company's adviser) must be careful not to

    A. receive performance-based fees
    B. enter into a contract with a customer that does not specifically spell out the compensation agreement
    C. refund commissions on mutual fund sales
    D. engage in any of the above activities

16. Which of the following fits the definition of "sale," according to the Uniform Securities Act?

    A. Solicitation of an offer to buy a security for value
    B. Attempt to dispose of a security for value
    C. Contract to dispose of a security
    D. Issuing a prospectus

17. Under the National Securities Markets Improvement Act and the Uniform Securities Act, if an investment adviser has custody of customer funds and securities, how often must the adviser send the customer a statement of account activity?

    A. Annually
    B. Quarterly
    C. Monthly
    D. With every transaction

18. Microscam wants to sell stock to the public. Six of Microscam's full-time employees sell the stock for Microscam. Under the Uniform Securities Act, these people would be considered

    A. broker-dealers
    B. agents of the issuer
    C. issuers
    D. agents of the broker-dealer

19. Under the Uniform Securities Act, which of the following is an example of a cease and desist order?

    A. Order that can be issued only by a federal agency to a brokerage firm to stop an advertising campaign
    B. Order by any administrative agency to refrain from a practice of business found by that agency to be unfair
    C. Order that can be issued only by the courts, requiring a business to stop an unfair practice
    D. Order from one brokerage firm to another brokerage firm to refrain from unfair business practices

20. The SEC can deny a person a license if the person

    I. has a criminal record
    II. has served jail time of one year or more
    III. has lost a civil lawsuit within the last year
    IV. was convicted of a crime but was given probation

    A. I and II
    B. I and III
    C. II and III
    D. III and IV

21. According to the Uniform Securities Act, if the registration of an agent is revoked by the administrator, the administrator can deny future registration of that agent as a(n)

    A. agent
    B. broker-dealer
    C. broker-dealer or agent
    D. The administrator has no authority to deny future registration.

22. Under the NSMIA, registered investment companies are required to file reports with the SEC

    A. more frequently
    B. quarterly
    C. semiannually
    D. annually

23. An elderly widow with no other income wishes to invest the proceeds from her husband's life insurance. According to the Uniform Securities Act, which of the following would be a suitable recommendation?

    A. Call options
    B. Municipal bonds
    C. Oil and gas exploration program that you know is going to strike
    D. Blue chip income stocks

24. You would be exempt from state registration as an investment adviser under the NSMIA and the USA if you had no place of business in the state and if, in any consecutive 12-month period, you executed trades for fewer than how many customers?

    A. Six
    B. Ten
    C. Fifteen
    D. Unlimited

25. Under the Uniform Securities Act, all of the following persons may provide investment advice incidental to their normal business without requiring registration as an investment adviser EXCEPT a(n)

    A. teacher
    B. economist
    C. lawyer
    D. engineer

26. As defined in the Uniform Securities Act, which of the following is NOT considered a security?

    A. Fixed annuity
    B. Stock option
    C. Limited partnership unit
    D. Commodity option

27. According to the Uniform Securities Act, from which of the following customers may an investment adviser borrow money?

    I. Affiliate of the investment adviser
    II. Broker-dealer
    III. Bank
    IV. Issuer of blue chip stock

    A. I, II and III
    B. I and IV
    C. II and III
    D. III

28. All of the following are exempt securities under the Uniform Securities Act EXCEPT

I. U.S. government securities
II. unsolicited transactions
III. transactions between issuers and underwriters
IV. securities of credit unions

A. I, II and IV
B. I and IV
C. II and III
D. IV

29. Under the Uniform Securities Act, which of the following is considered a broker-dealer?

I. Agent
II. Issuer
III. Corporation selling interests in an oil and gas limited partnership
IV. Credit union selling its own stock

A. I
B. I and III
C. II and IV
D. III

30. A partner in an issuing corporation effects transactions in the issuer's registered, non-exempt securities and receives a commission. Under the Uniform Securities Act, the partner is considered a(n)

A. agent
B. broker-dealer
C. investment adviser
D. issuer

31. With regard to the Uniform Securities Act, which of the following persons does NOT have to register as an investment adviser?

I. Broker-dealer who gives advice and charges a specific fee for that advice
II. Agent of a broker-dealer who gives investment advice within the course of his duties and charges a fee for that advice
III. Broker-dealer who gives investment advice that is incidental to the course of her business
IV. Attorney who writes a legal opinion of counsel for a municipal bond

A. I, II and IV only
B. III only
C. III and IV only
D. I, II, III and IV

32. According to the Uniform Securities Act, an investment adviser may have custody of a customer's funds and securities in which of the following circumstances?

A. If he has received the permission of the administrator
B. If custody is prohibited by the administrator
C. If he does not share in the capital gains of the account
D. If the administrator has been informed of the custody

33. Which of the following acts outlines the procedure for registering securities by coordination?

A. Securities Act of 1933
B. Securities Coordination Act of 1933
C. Uniform Securities Act
D. Trust Indenture Act of 1939

34. Which of the following statements are true?

    I. States cannot enforce recordkeeping and reporting responsibilities for state-registered investment advisers.
    II. States regulate investment advisers with less than $25 million in assets under management whose activity is largely concentrated within their boundaries.
    III. The SEC regulates investment advisers with $25 million or more in assets under management.
    IV. Only the SEC can enforce antifraud regulations against an investment adviser.

    A. I and III
    B. II and III
    C. III and IV
    D. I, II and IV

35. An agent's registration under the Uniform Securities Act must be renewed how frequently?

    A. Every 90 days
    B. Every December 31st
    C. Each state varies.
    D. Registration is effective until it is revoked, is withdrawn or expires.

36. According to the Uniform Securities Act, what must broker-dealers, state-registered investment advisers and agents provide the administrator as requirements for registration?

    I. Financial statements
    II. Consent to service of process
    III. Surety bonds
    IV. Updates of information during registration

    A. I and II only
    B. I and III only
    C. II only
    D. I, II, III and IV

37. According to the Uniform Securities Act, an agent could share in the profits of a customer's account in which of the following situations?

    I. The agent has written permission from the customer.
    II. The agent has written permission from the broker-dealer.
    III. The participation is proportional to the commission the agent receives.
    IV. The participation is proportional to the agent's investment in the account.

    A. I, II and IV only
    B. I and III only
    C. II and III only
    D. I, II, III and IV

38. According to the Uniform Securities Act, a person would be required to register as a broker-dealer in a state under which of the following circumstances?

    I. Person has no place of business in the state, but has directed offers to 25 residents of that state
    II. Person has no place of business in the state and deals exclusively with broker-dealers in that state
    III. Person has no place of business in the state and effects transactions exclusively with issuers of securities in that state
    IV. Person has a place of business in the state

    A. I, II and IV only
    B. I and IV only
    C. II and III only
    D. I, II, III and IV

39. An individual would NOT be considered an agent under the Uniform Securities Act if she engages in which of the following transactions?

    I. Isolated nonissuer transactions
    II. Transactions between an issuer and ordinary investors
    III. Transactions between an issuer and the underwriters
    IV. Transactions between an issuer and savings institutions or trust companies

    A. I, III and IV only
    B. II and III only
    C. II and IV only
    D. I, II, III and IV

40. A nonissuer corporation uses its employees to sell nonexempt securities. The corporation receives a commission on the sale of the securities. Some of the commission is then paid to the employees. According to the Uniform Securities Act, the corporation is a

    A. broker-dealer that must be registered
    B. corporation selling only to sophisticated investors
    C. broker-dealer engaging in exempt transactions
    D. corporation selling to an employee pension fund

41. According to the Uniform Securities Act, an example of an investment adviser is a

    A. lawyer
    B. publisher of a magazine
    C. person who is paid a fee for advising customers on securities
    D. person who is paid a commission for advising customers on securities

42. The definition of "investment company" excludes an investment pool

    A. that offers its securities to no more than 35 accredited investors
    B. that makes a public offering of its securities
    C. that purchases more than 25 percent of any registered investment company's securities
    D. whose securities are held exclusively by qualified purchasers (sophisticated investors)

43. As outlined in the Uniform Securities Act, an offer and sale does NOT exist if it is a(n)

    I. act as a result of a class vote by stockholders regarding a merger or consolidation
    II. bona fide pledge or loan
    III. act incident to a judicially approved reorganization in which a security is issued in exchange for one or more outstanding shares
    IV. act as a result of a judicially approved reorganization in which one security is issued in exchange for an outstanding security

    A. I and II only
    B. I, II and III only
    C. IV only
    D. I, II, III and IV

44. Under the Uniform Securities Act, the administrator has the power to require an agent licensee to

    A. have minimum net capital, post a surety bond and pass an exam
    B. post a surety bond and pass an exam
    C. post a surety bond, pay filing fees and pass an exam
    D. have minimum net capital, pay filing fees, pass an exam and post a surety bond

45. An agent representing a broker-dealer in Arkansas wishes to do business in Tennessee exclusively in the trading of certain exempt securities. Under the Uniform Securities Act, the agent would

    A. not have to register in Tennessee
    B. have to register in Tennessee
    C. not have to register if the broker-dealer were registered in Tennessee
    D. be allowed to do business because the securities are exempt

46. If it is in the public interest to do so, the Uniform Securities Act provides that the state administrator may deny the registration of a person for all of the following reasons EXCEPT that

    A. the applicant is not qualified owing to lack of experience
    B. a willful violation of the Uniform Securities Act has taken place
    C. the applicant is financially insolvent
    D. the applicant is enjoined temporarily from engaging in the securities business

47. Under the Uniform Securities Act, an agent's license is effective for

    A. one year, although each state may determine its own schedule for renewal
    B. 18 months, of which the first six months is a probationary period
    C. 20 years
    D. one year, with all registrations expiring on December 31st

48. All of the following are part of the registration by filing procedure under the Uniform Securities Act EXCEPT that

    A. companies must have attained a specific level of earnings for the prior three-year period
    B. a copy of the offering circular or prospectus must be filed
    C. if not denied, registration becomes effective after 30 days
    D. a statement must list the name(s) of the underwriter(s) and describe the terms of the offering

49. Under the Uniform Securities Act, no specific response is required from the state administrator before which of the following types of securities registration become effective?

    I. Coordination
    II. Qualification
    III. Filing
    IV. Mastication

    A. I and II only
    B. I and III only
    C. II and III only
    D. I, II, III and IV

50. All of the following statements are true regarding the selling of private placements under the Uniform Securities Act EXCEPT that

    A. they cannot be offered to more than 10 people in 12 consecutive months
    B. they cannot be offered to five people or more in 12 consecutive months
    C. the seller must reasonably believe that all buyers are purchasing for investment purposes only
    D. no commission or other remuneration is paid

◆ Answers & Rationale

1. **D.** An investment adviser may execute transactions through any firm, provided that the fee charged the customer is reasonable in comparison to the services provided. Potential conflicts of interest, such as when a transaction is executed through an affiliated broker-dealer, are subject to disclosure requirements.   (Page 39)

2. **B.** Answer B outlines the conditions under which a broker-dealer is considered an investment adviser. The antiques dealer provides advice on objects that are not considered securities; he therefore is not providing investment advice. Publishers may provide generic investment advice without being considered an investment adviser, and banks are excluded from the definition.   (Page 20)

3. **C.** As long as the agent sold the security with no intent to defraud, rescission may be offered. Rescission is the return of the customer's money, plus interest, less any income received from the investment.   (Page 10)

4. **D.** Under the scope of the Uniform Securities Act, if any part of a transaction occurs in a state, the entire transaction is under the jurisdiction of the state administrator.   (Page 8)

5. **B.** Sales of securities to financial institutions or accredited investors are exempt transactions.   (Page 62)

6. **B.** The states continue to receive filing fees from exempt issuers.   (Page 59)

7. **D.** The exception is selling rights. Choice I is stealing, choice II is failure to follow suitability standards and choice IV is fraudulent.   (Page 68)

8. **B.** Coordination is frequently used to register a security simultaneously under the Securities Act of 1933 and in a state. If the security's federal registration is pending and the administrator has received all of the required material, the two registrations can be declared effective at the same time.   (Page 56)

9. **D.** This statement is misleading under any circumstances. Under no circumstances can an agent promise profit in a security transaction.   (Page 64)

10. **D.** The advertising prospectus may now include performance data on the fund and would be subject to the SEC's reporting requirements. This data is added to the standardized information placed in a summary prospectus.   (Page 47)

11. **A.** An agent's license must be transferred immediately. Additionally, both the new and the old broker-dealer, as well as the agent, must notify the administrator of the transfer in writing.   (Page 14)

12. **A.** A qualified purchaser falls into one of the following categories: (1) individuals with $5 million in investments, (2) trusts sponsored by qualified purchasers, (3) family businesses wit $5 million or more invested or (4) business with no less than $25 million invested.   (Page 22)

13. **D.** The common requirements are to pay filing fees, post a surety bond and consent to service of process for all three of these designations. For broker-dealers and state-registered investment advisers, an additional net worth requirement has to be met.   (Page 26)

14. **D.** Under the NSMIA, the SEC will now be responsible for the improvement and oversight of market efficiency, competition in the securities industry and capital formation. The SEC is still responsible for acting in the public's best interest.   (Page 6)

15. **D.** All of these are violations under the Uniform Securities Act. Fees must be spelled out and can be either a flat fee or a percentage of the assets managed. Investment advisers of private

investment companies may receive performance-based fees.   (Page 35)

16. **C.** Solicitations and attempts to dispose are offers. Sales involve any contract or disposition for value.   (Page 3)

17. **B.** An investment adviser in possession of customer assets must send a statement to the customer every three months; the statement must list the securities held by the adviser and must show all transactions in the account since the last statement date.   (Page 34)

18. **B.** Microscam is the issuer. The definition of "agent" is any individual who works for others. If the employees are working for Microscam, they would be considered agents of the issuer.   (Page 12)

19. **B.** A cease and desist order is nothing more than an administrative agency telling you to stop what you are doing. The order can come from a federal, state or judicial body; it is not exclusive to any one.   (Page 10)

20. **A.** The SEC will now deny licensure to those persons with a criminal record who have served jail sentences of one year or more.   (Page 27)

21. **C.** Once registration has been revoked, the administrator can bar the registrant from ever again working in the securities business in any capacity.   (Page 9)

22. **A.** Management investment companies are now open to more frequent reporting requirements as deemed necessary by the SEC.   (Page 48)

23. **D.** This customer needs income. Of the answers given, the blue chip stocks would provide the highest level while still maintaining safety. The municipal bonds could be recommended if she had a tax problem, but she does not.   (Page 67)

24. **A.** Under the NSMIA and the USA, an investment adviser would be exempt from state registration requirements if he directed business communications in the state to fewer than six customers in a 12-month period. This is referred to as the "national de minimis."   (Page 25)

25. **B.** The Uniform Securities Act exempts from registration teachers, engineers, lawyers and accountants providing investment advice that is incidental to the performance of their normal business. Economists are not granted an exemption under the act.   (Page 21)

26. **A.** A fixed annuity is an insurance contract that cannot be traded for value. Commodity options (although not the underlying futures contracts) and stock options are considered securities, as are interests purchased in a limited partnership enterprise.   (Page 4)

27. **A.** An investment adviser may not borrow money from a customer unless the customer is an affiliate of the investment adviser, a broker-dealer, or a bank or another institution in the business of lending money.   (Page 67)

28. **C.** Government securities and securities of financial institutions are exempt securities. Unsolicited transactions and transactions between issuers and underwriters are exempt transactions, not exempt securities.   (Page 60)

29. **D.** "Broker-dealer" is defined as any person that invests for others or for his own account. A broker-dealer is not an issuer or an agent.   (Page 2)

30. **A.** Being a partner of an issuer does not automatically make you an agent unless you actively participate in the underwriting process and receive a commission for sales efforts.   (Page 12)

31. **C.** The key is "charges a fee" for the advice. Remember, attorneys are exempt from the definition of "investment adviser." (Page 21)

32. **D.** As long as retaining custody of funds is not prohibited, he may have custody of a customer's account after providing notice to the administrator.   (Page 34)

33. **A.** A security registered using coordination will coordinate that registration with the registration filed with the SEC. The Securities Act of 1933 is the basis for securities registration of securities sold interstate.   (Page 56)

34. **B.** Persons who have less than $25 million in assets under management must register on a state basis only. States as well as the SEC are required to enforce all antifraud regulations.
(Page 23)

35. **B.** Under the Uniform Securities Act, an agent's license expires annually on December 31st unless it is renewed.   (Page 12)

36. **C.** All three persons listed must provide a consent to service of process. Only broker-dealers and investment advisers are required to file financial statements and to provide updates of information. Only those broker-dealers, agents and advisers who have custody of or discretionary authority over customer securities may be required to post surety bonds.   (Page 13)

37. **A.** If an agent invests money with a customer, the agent may share in profits if the broker-dealer and the customer agree in writing and if the sharing is proportionate to the agent's investment. It has nothing to do with commissions.   (Page 69)

38. **B.** The term "broker-dealer" does not include a person who has no place of business in the state and who (1) effects transactions exclusively through issuers, other broker-dealers or institutions or (2) directs an offer in the state to an existing customer who is not a permanent resident of the state where the offer is received.
(Page 11)

39. **A.** An individual who effects securities transactions for compensation is defined as an agent. A person representing an issuer in an exempt transaction does not fall under the definition, nor does a person who represents an issuer in effecting transactions with existing employees in which no commissions are paid.   (Page 12)

40. **A.** A broker-dealer is in the business of effecting transactions in securities for its own account or for the accounts of others. Under the Uniform Securities Act, the broker-dealer must register in the state where business is transacted.
(Page 11)

41. **C.** The term "investment adviser" means any person who is in the business of selling investment advice.   (Page 20)

42. **D.** A qualified purchasers pool is an unregistered investment pool. Its purpose is to raise venture capital.   (Page 22)

43. **D.** The Uniform Securities Act specifically excludes these four choices from the definitions of "offer and sale."   (Page 3)

44. **C.** The administrator *may* require that, as a condition of registration, the agent post a surety bond, pay filing fees and take an examination that may be written, oral or both.   (Page 12)

45. **B.** Although the securities are exempted from registration, the agent must register in every state where business is attempted.   (Page 12)

46. **A.** Registration may be denied if the applicant willfully violates the Uniform Securities Act, is financially insolvent or has been enjoined from engaging in the securities business. If the person qualifies by virtue of training or knowledge, registration cannot be denied for lack of experience only.   (Page 15)

47. **D.** Registrations expire annually on December 31st unless renewed.   (Page 12)

48. **C.** Registration becomes effective after a five-day cooling-off period.   (Page 57)

49. **B.**   Registration by filing and coordination do not require a response from the state administrator for effectiveness. Registration by qualification, however, becomes effective only at the order of the administrator.   (Page 57)

50. **B.**   The Uniform Securities Act allows an exemption from registration for securities if they are sold to no more than 10 people (other than institutional investors), purchased for investment purposes and no commission is paid.   (Page 63)

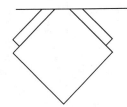

Appendix

Form ADV, Part II

OMB APPROVAL
OMB Number: 3235-0049
Expires: April 30, 2000
Estimated average burden
hours per response......9.01

FORM ADV
Part II · Page 1   **Uniform Application for Investment Adviser Registration**

Name of Investment Adviser:					
Address:	(Number and Street)	(City)	State)	(Zip Code)	Area Code: Telephone Number: ( )

This part of Form ADV gives information about the investment adviser and its business for the use of clients.
The information has not been approved or verified by any governmental authority.

Table of Contents

(Schedules A, B, C, D, and E are included with Part I of this Form, for the use of regulatory bodies, and are not distributed to clients.)

Potential persons who are to respond to the collection of information contained in this form are not required to respond unless the
form displays a currently valid OMB control number.

FORM ADV Part II- Page 2	Applicant:	SEC File Number: 801-	Date:

Definitions for Part II

Related person — Any officer, director or partner of applicant or any person directly or indirectly controlling, controlled by, or under common control with the applicant, including any non-clerical, non-ministerial employee.

Investment Supervisory Services — Giving continuous investment advice to a client (or making investments for the client) based on the individual needs of the client. Individual needs include, for example, the nature of other client assets and the client's personal and family obligations.

---

1. **A. Advisory Services and Fees.** (check the applicable boxes)

   Applicant:

   For each type of service provided, state the approximate % of total advisory billings from that service. (See instruction below.)

   ☐ (1) Provides investment supervisory services .... _____ %
   ☐ (2) Manages investment advisory accounts not involving investment supervisory services .... _____ %
   ☐ (3) Furnishes investment advice through consultations not included in either service described above .... _____ %
   ☐ (4) Issues periodicals about securities by subscription .... _____ %
   ☐ (5) Issues special reports about securities not included in any service described above .... _____ %
   ☐ (6) Issues, not as part of any service described above, any charts, graphs, formulas, or other devices which clients may use to evaluate securities .... _____ %
   ☐ (7) On more than an occasional basis, furnishes advice to clients on matters not involving securities .... _____ %
   ☐ (8) Provides a timing service... _____ %
   ☐ (9) Furnishes advice about securities in any manner not described above .... _____ %

   (Percentages should be based on applicant's last fiscal year. If applicant has not completed its first fiscal year, provide estimates of advisory billings for that year and state that the percentages are estimates.)

   B. Does applicant call any of the services it checked above financial planning or some similar term? .... Yes ☐ No ☐

   C. Applicant offers investment advisory services for: (check all that apply)

   ☐ (1) A percentage of assets under management   ☐ (4) Subscription fees
   ☐ (2) Hourly charges   ☐ (5) Commissions
   ☐ (3) Fixed fees (not including subscription fees) ☐ (6) Other

   ---

   D. For each checked box in A above, describe on Schedule F:

   - the services provided, including the name of any publication or report issued by the adviser on a subscription basis or for a fee

   - applicant's basic fee schedule, how fees are charged and whether its fees are negotiable

   - when compensation is payable, and if compensation is payable before service is provided, how a client may get a refund or may terminate an investment advisory contract before its expiration date

---

2. **Types of Clients** — Applicant generally provides investment advice to: (check those that apply)

   ☐ A. Individuals   ☐ E. Trusts, estates, or charitable organizations

   ☐ B. Banks or thrift institutions   ☐ F. Corporations or business entities other than those listed above

   ☐ C. Investment companies

   ☐ D. Pension and profit sharing plans   ☐ G. Other (describe on Schedule F)

Answer all items. Complete amended pages in full, circle amended items and file with execution page (page 1).

FORM ADV	Applicant:	SEC File Number:	Date:
Part II- Page 3		801-	

3. **Types of Investments.** Applicant offers advice on the following: (check those that apply)

A. Equity Securities

☐ (1) exchange-listed securities
☐ (2) securities traded over-the-counter
☐ (3) foreign issuers

☐ B. Warrants

☐ C. Corporate debt securities
(other than commercial paper)

☐ D. Commercial paper

☐ E. Certificates of deposit

☐ F. Municipal securities

G. Investment company securities:
☐ (1) variable life insurance
☐ (2) variable annuities
☐ (3) mutual fund shares

☐ H. Unites States government securities

I. Options contracts on:
☐ (1) securities
☐ (2) commodities

J. Futures contracts on:
☐ (1) tangibles
☐ (2) intangibles

K. Interests in partnerships investing in:
☐ (1) real estate
☐ (2) oil and gas interests
☐ (3) other (explain on Schedule F)

☐ L. Other (explain on Schedule F)

4. **Methods of Analysis, Sources of Information, and Investment Strategies.**

A. Applicant's security analysis methods include: (check those that apply)

(1) ☐ Charting

(2) ☐ Fundamental

(3) ☐ Technical

(4) ☐ Cyclical

(5) ☐ Other (explain on Schedule F)

B. The main sources of information applicant uses include: (check those that apply)

(1) ☐ Financial newspapers and magazines

(2) ☐ Inspections of corporate activities

(3) ☐ Research materials prepared by others

(4) ☐ Corporate rating services

(5) ☐ Timing services

(6) ☐ Annual reports, prospectuses, filings with the Securities and Exchange Commission

(7) ☐ Company press releases

(8) ☐ Other (explain on Schedule F)

C. The investment strategies used to implement any investment advice given to clients include: (check those that apply)

(1) ☐ Long term purchases
(securities held at least a year)

(2) ☐ Short term purchases
(securities sold within a year)

(3) ☐ Trading (securities sold within 30 days)

(4) ☐ Short sales

(5) ☐ Margin transactions

(6) ☐ Option writing, including covered options, uncovered options or spreading strategies

(7) ☐ Other (explain on Schedule F)

Answer all items. Complete amended pages in full, circle amended items and file with execution page (page 1).

FORM ADV Part II · Page 4	Applicant:	SEC File Number: 801-	Date:

---

5. Education and Business Standards.

Are there any general standards of education or business experience that applicant requires of those involved in determining or giving investment advice to clients? .... Yes ☐ No ☐

(If yes, describe these standards on Schedule F.)

---

6. Education and Business Background.

For:

- each member of the investment committee or group that determines general investment advice to be given to clients, or

- if the applicant has no investment committee or group, each individual who determines general investment advice given to clients (if more than five, respond only for their supervisors)

- each principal executive officer of applicant or each person with similar status or performing similar functions.

On Schedule F, give the:

- name
- year of birth
- formal education after high school
- business background for the preceding five years

---

7. Other Business Activities. (check those that apply)

☐ A. Applicant is actively engaged in a business other than giving investment advice.

☐ B. Applicant sells products or services other than investment advice to clients.

☐ C. The principal business of applicant or its principal executive officers involves something other than providing investment advice.

(For each checked box describe the other activities, including the time spent on them, on Schedule F.)

---

8. Other Financial Industry Activities or Affiliations. (check those that apply)

☐ A. Applicant is registered (or has an application pending) as a securities broker-dealer.

☐ B. Applicant is registered (or has an application pending) as a futures commission merchant, commodity pool operator or commodity trading adviser.

C. Applicant has arrangements that are material to its advisory business or its clients with a related person who is a:

☐ (1) broker-dealer   ☐ (7) accounting firm

☐ (2) investment company   ☐ (8) law firm

☐ (3) other investment adviser   ☐ (9) insurance company or agency

☐ (4) financial planning firm   ☐ (10) pension consultant

☐ (5) commodity pool operator, commodity trading   ☐ (11) real estate broker or dealer
      adviser or futures commission merchant

                                              ☐ (12) entity that creates or packages limited partnerships

☐ (6) banking or thrift institution

(For each checked box in C, on Schedule F identify the related person and describe the relationship and the arrangements.)

D. Is applicant or a related person a general partner in any partnership in which clients are solicited to invest? .... Yes ☐ No ☐

(If yes, describe on Schedule F the partnerships and what they invest in.)

Answer all items. Complete amended pages in full, circle amended items and file with execution page (page 1).

FORM ADV	Applicant:	SEC File Number:	Date:
Part II - Page 5		801-	

9. **Participation or Interest in Client Transactions.**

Applicant or a related person: (check those that apply)

☐ A. As principal, buys securities for itself from or sells securities it owns to any client.

☐ B. As broker or agent effects securities transactions for compensation for any client.

☐ C. As broker or agent for any person other than a client effects transactions in which client securities are sold to or bought from a brokerage customer.

☐ D. Recommends to clients that they buy or sell securities or investment products in which the applicant or a related person has some financial interest.

☐ E. Buys or sells for itself securities that it also recommends to clients.

(For each box checked, describe on Schedule F when the applicant or a related person engages in these transactions and what restrictions, internal procedures, or disclosures are used for conflicts of interest in those transactions.)

10. **Conditions for Managing Accounts.** Does the applicant provide investment supervisory services, manage investment advisory accounts or hold itself out as providing financial planning or some similarly termed services *and* impose a minimum dollar value of assets or other conditions for starting or maintaining an account?. . . . .

Yes   No
☐   ☐

(If yes, describe on Schedule F.)

11. **Review of Accounts.** If applicant provides investment supervisory services, manages investment advisory accounts, or holds itself out as providing financial planning or some similarly termed services:

A. Describe below the reviews and reviewers of the accounts. **For reviews,** include their frequency, different levels, and triggering factors. **For reviewers,** include the number of reviewers, their titles and functions, instructions they receive from applicant on performing reviews, and number of accounts assigned each.

B. Describe below the nature and frequency of regular reports to clients on their accounts.

Answer all items. Complete amended pages in full, circle amended items and file with execution page (page 1).

FORM ADV
Part II · Page 6

| Applicant: | SEC File Number: 801- | Date: |

---

12. Investment or Brokerage Discretion.

A. Does applicant or any related person have authority to determine, without obtaining specific client consent, the:

(1) securities to be bought or sold? .... Yes ☐ No ☐

(2) amount of the securities to be bought or sold? .... Yes ☐ No ☐

(3) broker or dealer to be used? .... Yes ☐ No ☐

(4) commission rates paid? .... Yes ☐ No ☐

B. Does applicant or a related person suggest brokers to clients? .... Yes ☐ No ☐

For each yes answer to A describe on Schedule F any limitations on the authority. For each yes to A(3), A(4) or B, describe on Schedule F the factors considered in selecting brokers and determining the reasonableness of their commissions. If the value of products, research and services given to the applicant or a related person is a factor, describe:

• the products, research and services

• whether clients may pay commissions higher than those obtainable from other brokers in return for those products and services

• whether research is used to service all of applicant's accounts or just those accounts paying for it; and

• any procedures the applicant used during the last fiscal year to direct client transactions to a particular broker in return for products and research services received.

13. Additional Compensation.

Does the applicant or a related person have any arrangements, oral or in writing, where it:

A. is paid cash by or receives some economic benefit (including commissions, equipment or non-research services) from a non-client in connection with giving advice to clients? .... Yes ☐ No ☐

B. directly or indirectly compensates any person for client referrals? .... Yes ☐ No ☐

(For each yes, describe the arrangements on Schedule F.

14. Balance Sheet. Applicant must provide a balance sheet for the most recent fiscal year on Schedule G if applicant:

• has custody of client funds or securities; or

• requires prepayment of more than $500 in fees per client and 6 or more months in advance

Has applicant provided a Schedule G balance sheet? .... Yes ☐ No ☐

Answer all items. Complete amended pages in full, circle amended items and file with execution page (page 1).

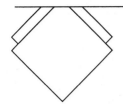

Glossary

accredited investor As defined in Rule 502 of Regulation D, any institution or individual meeting minimum net worth requirements for the purchase of securities qualifying under the Regulation D registration exemption.

An accredited investor generally is accepted to be one who:

- has a net worth of $1 million or more; or
- has had an annual income of $200,000 or more in each of the two most recent years (or $300,000 jointly with a spouse) and who has a reasonable expectation of reaching the same income level in the current year.

administrator (1) A person authorized by a court of law to liquidate the estate of an intestate decedent. (2) The official or agency administering the securities laws of a state.

advertisement Any material designed for use by newspapers, magazines, radio, television, telephone recording or any other public medium to solicit business. The firm using advertising has little control over the type of individuals being exposed to the advertising. *See also* sales literature.

advertising prospectus An investment company prospectus that includes the fund's performance data, as well as standardized information contained in the summary prospectus.

advisory board Under the Investment Company Act of 1940, a board that advises an investment company on matters concerning its investments in securities, but that does not have the power to make investment decisions or take action itself. An advisory board must be composed of persons who have no other connection with, and serve no other function for, the investment company.

affiliate Any person directly or indirectly owning, controlling or holding, with power to vote, 10 percent or more of the outstanding voting securities of another person; also, any officer, director or partner of another entity for which such person acts in such capacity.

When used with respect to a member or sponsor, "affiliate" means any person who controls, is controlled by or is under control with such member or sponsor and includes:

- any partner, officer or director (or any person performing similar functions) of such member or sponsor, or a person who beneficially owns 50 percent or more of the equity interest in, or who has the power to vote 50 percent or more of the voting interest in, such member or sponsor; or
- any person who beneficially owns or has the right to acquire 10 percent or more of the equity interest in, or who has the power to vote 10 percent or more of the voting interest in, such member or sponsor, or a person who beneficially owns 50 percent or more of the voting interest in, or who has the power to vote 50 percent or more of the voting interest in, such member or sponsor.

agent (1) An individual acting for the accounts of others; also, any person licensed by a state as a life insurance agent. (*Syn.* broker) (2) A securities salesperson who represents a broker-dealer or an issuer when selling or trying to sell securities to the investing public. This individual is considered an agent whether he actually receives or simply solicits orders. In other words, an agent is anyone who receives an order while representing a broker-dealer.

assignment (1) A document accompanying or part of a stock certificate that is signed by the person named on the certificate for the purpose of transferring the certificate's title to another person's name. (2) The act of identifying and notifying an account holder that an option held short in that account has been exercised by the option owner.

associated person of a member (AP) Any employee, manager, director, officer or partner of a member broker-dealer or another entity (issuer, bank, etc.) or any person controlling, controlled by or in common control with that member is considered an associated person of that member.

blue-sky To qualify a securities offering in a particular state.

blue-sky laws The nickname for state regulations governing the securities industry.

broker (1) An individual or a firm that charges a fee or commission for executing buy and sell orders submitted by another individual or firm. (2) The role of a broker firm when it acts as an agent for a customer and charges the customer a commission for its services.

broker-dealer (1) An individual or a firm that charges a fee or commission for executing buy and sell orders submitted by another individual or firm. (2) The role of a broker firm when it acts as an agent for a customer and charges the customer a commission for its services.

The term "broker-dealer" is defined in the Uniform Securities Act so that it can be determined who must register in the state as a broker-dealer. If the person does not fall under the definition of "broker-dealer" as defined by the law, the registration process is not necessary.

The following persons are not classified as broker-dealers:
- agents (registered representatives);
- issuers;
- banks, savings institutions or trust companies;
- persons who have no place of business in the state and who: (a) effect securities transactions in the state exclusively through the issuers of the securities, other broker-dealers or financial institutions (banks, savings institutions, trust companies, insurance companies and investment companies) or
(b) directs an offer in this state to an existing customer who has less than 30 days' temporary residency in the state where the offer is received.

dealer The role of a brokerage firm when it acts as a principal in a particular trade. A firm is acting as a dealer when it buys or sells a security for its own account and at its own risk and then charges the customer a markup or markdown. Any person who is engaged in the business of buying and selling securities for her own account either directly or through a broker, and who is not a bank, is considered a dealer. (*Syn.* principal)

discretion The authority for someone other than the beneficial owner of an account to make investment decisions for that account regarding the security, the number of shares or units and whether to buy or sell. Decisions concerning only timing and price do not constitute "discretion."

exempt security A security exempt from the registration requirements (although not from the antifraud requirements) of the Securities Act of 1933 (e.g., U.S. government and municipal securities).

exempt transaction A transaction exempt from registration and advertising requirements under the Uniform Securities Act. Examples of exempt transactions include:
- isolated nonissuer transactions;
- nonissuer transactions in outstanding securities (normal market trading);
- transactions with financial institutions (banks, savings institutions, trust companies, insurance companies, pension or profit-sharing plans, broker-dealers, etc.);
- unsolicited transactions;
- fiduciary transactions;
- private placement transactions;
- transactions between an issuer and its underwriters; and
- transactions with an issuer's employees, partners or directors if no commission is paid directly or indirectly for the soliciting.

Exemption from the act's registration and advertising requirements does not mean that a transaction is exempt from the act's antifraud provisions.

fidelity bond *See* surety bond.

fiduciary A person legally appointed and authorized to represent another person and act on her behalf.

fraud The deliberate concealment, misrepresentation or omission of material information or the truth to deceive or manipulate another party for unlawful or unfair gain.

government security An obligation of the U.S. government, backed by the full faith and credit of the government, and regarded as the highest grade or safest issue (i.e., default risk-free). The U.S. government issues short-term Treasury bills, medium-term Treasury notes and long-term Treasury bonds.

guaranteed Securities that have a guarantee, usually from a source other than the issuer, as to the payment of principal, interest or dividends.

inside information Material and nonpublic information obtained or used by a person for the purpose of trading in securities.

insider Any person who has nonpublic knowledge (material information) about a corporation. Insiders include directors, officers and stockholders who own more than 10 percent of any class of equity security of a corporation.

institutional account An account held for the benefit of others. Examples include banks, trusts, pension and profit-sharing plans, mutual funds and insurance companies.

institutional investor A person or an organization that trades securities in large enough share quantities or dollar amounts that it qualifies for preferential treatment and lower trade costs (commissions). Institutional investors are covered by fewer protective regulations because it is assumed that they are more knowledgeable and better able to protect themselves.

investment adviser Any person who, for compensation (a flat fee or a percentage of assets managed), offers investment advice. For investment companies, the adviser has the day-to-day responsibility of investing the cash and securities held in a mutual fund's portfolio. The adviser must adhere to the objectives as stated in the fund's prospectus. This definition includes persons who issue written reports or analyses for compensation. The term "investment adviser" does not include:

- institutions such as banks, savings institutions or trust companies;
- professionals such as lawyers, accountants or teachers whose performance of these services is solely incidental to the practice of their profession;
- broker-dealers that offer investment portfolio advice as part of their business of being broker-dealers and that receive no special compensation for that service;
- publishers of any financial publication of general, regular and paid circulation; however, a person who sells subscriptions to investment advisory publications (market letters) is considered an investment adviser under the Uniform Securities Act;
- persons whose investment advice relates only to U.S. government securities and certain municipal securities; and
- persons having no place of business within the state and whose activities are limited to (a) professional clients (institutions) or (b) a very few solicitations or sales to clients other than those mentioned above. For instance, some states limit this activity to less than six clients in any 12 consecutive months.

The term "investment adviser" also excludes any person that the state administrator of the Uniform Securities Act decides not to include.

investment adviser representative Any partner, officer, director or other individual employed by or associated with an investment adviser who (1) gives investment advice or makes recommendations, (2) manages client accounts or portfolios, (3) determines which investment recommendations or advice should be given, (4) offers or sells investment advisory services or (5) supervises employees involved in any of these activities.

Investment Advisers Act of 1940 Legislation passed by Congress that requires all investment advisers to register as such with the SEC and to abide by the Investment Advisers Act of 1940 and all other applicable federal acts.

investment company A company engaged primarily in the business of investing and trading in securities, including face-amount certificate companies, unit investment trusts and management companies.

Investment Company Act of 1940 Congressional legislation enacted to regulate investment companies that requires any investment company in interstate commerce to register with the SEC.

issuer (1) The corporation or municipality that offers its securities for sale; also, the creator of an option (the issuer of an over-the-counter option is the option writer, and the issuer of a listed option is the Options Clearing Corporation). (2) According to the Uniform Securities Act, any person who issues or proposes to issue any security.

When a corporation or municipality raises additional capital through an offering of securities, that corporation or municipality is the issuer of those securities. An issuer transaction also is called a *primary transaction.*

There are two exceptions to the basic definition of "issuer." In the case of voting-trust certificates or collateral-trust certificates, the term "issuer" refers to the person who assumes the duties of depositor or manager. There is considered to be no issuer for certificates of interest or participation in oil, gas, or mining titles or leases where payments are made out of production.

market maker (principal) A dealer willing to accept the risk of holding securities to facilitate trading in a particular security(ies).

municipal security A debt security issued by a state, a municipality or another subdivision (such as a school, a park, or a sanitary or some other local taxing district) to raise money to finance its capital expenditures. Such expenditures might include the construction of highways, public works or school buildings.

net capital Liquid capital (cash and assets readily convertible into cash) maintained by a broker-dealer.

nonissuer A person other than the issuer of a security. In a nonissuer securities transaction, for example, the issuer is not one of the parties in the transaction, and the transaction therefore is not, according to the law, directly or indirectly for the benefit of the issuer.

When the Uniform Securities Act refers to a *nonissuer transaction,* it is referring to a transaction in which the proceeds of the sale go to the selling stockholder. For example, a trade of 100 shares of RCA on the New York Stock Exchange is a typical nonissuer transaction. Most nonissuer transactions also are called *secondary transactions.*

offer (1) An indication by an investor, a trader or a dealer of a willingness to sell a security or commodity. (2) Under the Uniform Securities Act, every attempt to solicit a purchase or sale in a security for value.

person An individual, a corporation, a partnership, an association, a fund, a joint stock company, an unincorporated organization, a trust in which the interests of the beneficiaries are evidenced by a security, a government or a political subdivision of a government.

private investment company An unregistered investment company whose investment objective is to raise capital for business ventures. Qualified purchasers are eligible to invest in private investment companies.

private placement An offering that complies with Regulation D (Rule 505 and Rule 506); generally, the offer of an unregistered security to no more than 35 nonaccredited investors or to an unlimited number of accredited investors. The Uniform Securities Act's private placement provision allows an exemption from full state registration for a security that is sold in that state to no more than 10 nonaccredited investors.

prospectus The legal document that must be given to every investor who purchases registered securities in an offering. It describes the details of the company and the particular offering. (*Syn.* final prospectus)

qualified purchaser A sophisticated investor who invests in a private investment company. This includes:

- an individual with $5 million or more invested;
- a family-owned business with $5 million or more invested;
- a trust established by qualified purchasers; and
- a company that invests on a discretionary basis a minimum of $25 million in investments.

registered investment company An investment company, such as an open-end management company (mutual fund) or closed-end management company, that is registered with the SEC and exempt from state registration and regulation.

registered representative For NASD registration and exam and licensing purposes, refers to all associated persons engaged in the investment banking and securities business. This includes:

- assistant officers (who are not principals);
- individuals who supervise, solicit or conduct business in securities; and
- individuals who train people to supervise, solicit or conduct business in securities.

Anyone who is not a principal and not engaged in clerical or brokerage administration is subject to registration and exam licensing as a registered representative—except for foreign associates. (*Syn.* account executive, stockbroker)

registration by coordination A security is eligible for blue-sky registration by coordination in a state if the issuer files for registration of that security under the Securities Act of 1933 and files duplicates of the registration documents with the state administrator. The state registration becomes effective at the same time the federal registration statement becomes effective.

registration by filing A security is eligible for blue-sky registration by filing in a state if the issuer files for registration of that security under the Securities Act of 1933, meets minimum net worth and other requirements, and notifies the state of this eligibility by filing certain documents with the state administrator. The state registration becomes effective at the same time the federal registration statement becomes effective.

registration by qualification A security is eligible for blue-sky registration by qualification in a state if the issuer files registration documents for that security with the state administrator; meets minimum net worth, disclosure and other requirements; and files appropriate registration fees. The state registration becomes effective when the administrator so orders.

registration statement Before nonexempt securities can be offered to the public, they require registration under the Securities Act of 1933. The registration statement must disclose all pertinent information concerning the issuer and the offering. This statement is submitted to the SEC in accordance with the requirements of the 1933 act.

sales literature Any written material used to help sell a product and distributed by the firm in a controlled manner.

Securities Act of 1933 The federal legislation requiring the full and fair disclosure of all material information about the issuance of new securities.

Securities and Exchange Commission (SEC) The commission, created by Congress to protect investors, that enforces the Securities Act of 1933, the Securities Exchange Act of 1934, the Trust Indenture Act of 1939, the Investment Company Act of 1940, the Investment Advisers Act of 1940 and other securities laws.

Securities Exchange Act of 1934 The federal legislation establishing the Securities and Exchange Commission that regulates securities exchanges and over-the-counter markets and that protects investors from unfair and inequitable practices.

securities information processor A person who is in the business of providing information about securities transactions or quotations on a current and continuing basis. The information may be published on paper (such as in the *Pink Sheets*) or it may be disseminated through a computer network. Specifically excluded from the definition are persons who handle such information on a regular basis in the course of their business activities but who are not "in the business" of doing so.

security Under the act of 1934, any note, stock, bond, investment contract, debenture, certificate of interest in profit-sharing or partnership agreement, certificate of deposit, collateral trust certificate, preorganization certificate, option on a security or other instrument of investment commonly known as a *security*.

Also categorized as securities are interests in oil and gas drilling programs, real estate condominiums and cooperatives, farmland or animals, commodity option contracts, whiskey warehouse receipts, multilevel distributorship arrangements and merchandising marketing programs.

The accurate determination of what is a security is crucial to registered representatives con-

ducting their activities in compliance with state securities laws. In general, "security" can be defined as any piece of securitized paper that can be traded for value, except an insurance policy or a fixed annuity. As established by the federal courts, the basic test for determining whether a specific investment falls within the definition of "security" is whether the investor invests his money in a common enterprise and is led to expect profits from the managerial efforts of the promoter or a third party.

self-regulatory organization (SRO) An entity that is accountable to the SEC for the enforcement of federal securities laws, as well as for the supervision of securities practices, within an assigned field of jurisdiction. Eight SROs function under the oversight of the Commission. Selected jurisdictions include the:

- New York Stock Exchange (NYSE). All matters related to trading in NYSE-listed securities and the conduct of NYSE member firms and associated persons.
- National Association of Securities Dealers (NASD). All matters related to investment banking (securities underwriting), trading in the over-the-counter market and the conduct of NASD member firms and associated persons.
- Municipal Securities Rulemaking Board (MSRB). All matters related to the underwriting and trading of state and municipal securities.
- Chicago Board Options Exchange (CBOE). All matters related to the writing and trading of standardized options and related contracts listed on that exchange.

sell The act of conveying ownership of a security or other property for money or other value; every contract to sell a security or an interest in a security. Sales include the following:

- Any security given or delivered with, or as a bonus for, any purchase of securities is considered to have been offered and sold for value.
- A gift of assessable stock is considered to involve an offer and sale.
- Every sale or offer of a warrant or right to purchase or subscribe to another security is considered to include an offer of the other security.

Sales do not include bona fide pledges or loans, or stock dividends if nothing of value is given by the stockholders for the dividend.

surety bond (1) A bond required by NYSE Rule 319 for all employees, officers and partners of member firms to protect clients against acts of misplacement, fraudulent trading and check forgery. (2) The blanket surety bond that indemnifies against losses due to check forgery, lost securities or fraudulent trading that every member firm required to join the Securities Investor Protection Corporation (that is, any firm doing business with the public) must purchase and maintain. (*Syn.* fidelity bond)

transfer agent A person or an organization responsible for recording the names of registered stockholders and the number of shares owned, seeing that the certificates are signed by the appropriate corporate officers, affixing the corporate seal and delivering the securities to the transferee.

underwriter The entity responsible for marketing stocks, bonds, mutual fund shares and so on.

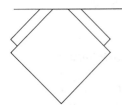

Index

Notes

Notes